Edelstein, Jillian.
Truth & lies : stories
from the Truth and
2002, c2001
33305201828039
MH   04/25/02

WITHDRAWN

D0689425

TRUTH & LIES

Stories from the Truth and Reconciliation Commission in South Africa

JILLIAN EDELSTEIN

With an Introduction by **Michael Ignatieff** and an essay by **Pumla Gobodo-Madikizela**

THE NEW PRESS

SANTA CLARA COUNTY LIBRARY

▪ 3 3305 20182 8039

During my lifetime I have dedicated myself to this struggle of the African people.
I have fought against white domination, and I have fought against black domination. I have
cherished the ideal of a democratic and free society in which all persons live together in
harmony and with equal opportunities. It is an ideal which I hope to live for and to achieve.
But if needs be, it is an ideal for which I am prepared to die.

Nelson Mandela, 20 April 1964

TRUTH&LIES

Stories from the Truth and Reconciliation Commission in South Africa

JILLIAN EDELSTEIN

With an Introduction by Michael Ignatieff and an essay by Pumla Gobodo-Madikizela

FOREWORD BY **JILLIAN EDELSTEIN**

INTRODUCTION BY **MICHAEL IGNATIEFF**

ESSAY BY **PUMLA GOBODO-MADIKIZELA**

Opening photographs: Cradock, Eastern Cape, p3; Upington, Northern Cape, p4–5; Meadowlands, Soweto, p6–7; Crossroads, Cape Town p8–9; all 2000. Opposite: Early morning workers leaving the resettlement camp at Onverwacht (which means 'Unexpected'), near Bloemfontein, Orange Free State, 1984

FOREWORD JILLIAN EDELSTEIN

One of the first events I ever photographed, while I was still a student at the University of Cape Town, was the demolition of the Crossroads squatter camp by the police in 1977. It was winter. The bulldozers were rolling over the tin shacks and the homeless squatters had made a futile protest by throwing their possessions on to the main road in front of the camp. The police and their dogs were trying to control the angry crowd. This was just one local event which epitomized the increasing repression by the state. It heralded the violent confrontations between the liberation movements and the apartheid regime in the next decade.

I became a press photographer in the Johannesburg area at the beginning of the 1980s. Growing up white in apartheid South Africa entitled one to massive and instant privilege. It led to complicated emotions—among them anger and guilt. Photography was a way, for me, of channelling those emotions. At that time I believed that by pointing a camera at security police, or at Casspirs (armoured personnel carriers) cruising the townships, or by documenting clashes between protestors and riot police I might help to change the situation in our country.

In 1985 I left South Africa to take up a photography course in London. After that, although I went back regularly to visit my family, I was relegated to watching most of the political events as they unfolded on television. Back in South Africa for my sister's wedding in 1996, I was gripped by the TV footage of the early scenes from the Truth Commission. I promised myself I would return to document the process.

Over the next four years I went back and forth between England and South Africa covering the hearings, but I was always aware that it would be impossible to attend every hearing in every small town and every city in every province around the country. There are many people who testified before the TRC who are not in this book. I did what I could. I knew the contradictions and the controversies that raged around the Truth Commission right from the start. But nothing prepared me for the emotional world within the community halls and courtrooms in which we observers witnessed the testimonies and confessions of the victims and perpetrators where truth gave way to lies and lies gave way to truth.

I often pondered over why people agreed to be photographed. For the victims, I guessed it might have been because they wanted to reclaim their dignity, their past, or to feel acknowledged for the part they had played. Largely it seemed to me they were grateful to have had the opportunity to share their experiences and to make public their painful stories. Perhaps this process of being in front of the camera was part of that ritual. It was harder to comprehend why the perpetrators offered themselves up so willingly for a portrait, often proudly, as if they had played some heroic part in South Africa's history.

Wherever I went I came across people dealing with tumultuous emotions. In KwaZulu/Natal, after the hearings into Inkatha-ANC violence, I met Mrs Msweli who showed me the forest where her son had been murdered; it was a strange and difficult thing to share that place with her. I felt her generosity and her pain. And I tried to show her dignity and the strength in her suffering.

I failed to persuade a number of 'key players' to be photographed. I had many telephone conversations with Joe Mamasela, a black security policeman who had turned state's witness. He even enticed me to fly from Cape Town to Johannesburg to photograph him. When I arrived his cell phone was switched off. I never reached him again. I faxed innumerable requests to Winnie Madikizela-Mandela. She had the knack of responding to them some weeks after I had left town. When I eventually got P. W. Botha on the line he said I should respect his privacy and directed me to the archive which housed his history.

It was strange to come face to face with a man like Dirk Coetzee, whose actions epitomized the atrocities of the apartheid regime, and there he was all smiling and sweet and charming, offering me English Breakfast tea with his gun strapped to his wrist. Good and evil are simple concepts, but they can wear all kinds of disguises.

There are many South Africans who refused to co-operate with the Truth Commission and many who should have been held responsible who will never have to account for their actions. Questions were evaded and the truth distorted. Perhaps this is best illustrated by the ex-President, Willem de Klerk, who, questioned at the TRC hearing into human rights abuses committed by members of the state forces during his term of office, said: 'Can I, before I reply to the question, just make the point that I don't think that one could accept, as the truth and the whole truth and nothing but the truth, each and every statement made by each and every person applying for amnesty.'

The Amnesty Committee's proceedings were extended over and over again. The verdicts remain controversial. The whole process has finally ended, the offices closed down, the staff dispersed. In general, the success of this long term project in South Africa's history remains questionable, but it is hard to think that for many individuals it has not been invaluable. Joyce Mtimkulu, who discovered that her son, Siphiwo, had been shot and detained, poisoned by the security police, released, kidnapped again and finally killed, seemed to speak for many when she told me, after listening to the testimonies of those responsible, 'at least now we know what happened'.

INTRODUCTION MICHAEL IGNATIEFF

Since its report came out in 1998, the South African Truth and Reconciliation Commission has become a model for other societies seeking to rebuild their ethical order and reckon with the past. An academic field—'transitional justice'—has arisen to contrast the different ways societies seek healing and justice after periods of war or tyranny.[1] There are many ways to do this: the de-Nazification of West Germany after 1945 followed by the de-Stasification of East Germany after 1989, the Chilean, Salvadorean and Argentinian truth commissions, the international tribunals in The Hague and Arusha, the indictment of Pinochet. In all these processes, the essential problem is how to balance peace and justice, forgetting and forgiving, healing and punishment, truth and reconciliation. Of all the attempts to balance these competing claims, pride of place always goes to South Africa. It remains the template, the most ambitious and far-reaching of the attempts at catharsis and justice.

The photographs in Jillian Edelstein's collection remind us that the South African experience was one of a kind, and they remind us, by implication, that all such processes are unique. Only South Africa had apartheid. Only South Africa had the African National Congress. Only South Africa had Nelson Mandela. Only South Africa had Desmond Tutu and Alex Boraine. Most of all, as Jillian Edelstein's photographs show, only South Africa had the people of the townships.

The great thing about fine photography is that it prevents abstraction. Jillian Edelstein's pictures take us back to the way it really was: the municipal halls, the men and women listening to the testimony on earphones in Xhosa, Afrikaans or English; the witness protection experts with their side arms, the bleakly unchanging world of South African injustice just outside. All of this detail is essential to any understanding of what abstractions like truth, justice and reconciliation actually mean. Jillian Edelstein has preserved the reality of the process so that we will remember that truth and reconciliation were the work of individuals, who refused to live with silence, with lies, with equivocations and excuses. But it was never just an individual process either. Truth and reconciliation depended on immense and widely diffused political awareness that such a process was necessary if the country was to have any kind of future at all.

Outsiders have been sentimental about the South African process, as they have been about Nelson Mandela, the rainbow nation and so on. Everyone likes to watch catharsis, especially if it is someone else's. For insiders, citizens of South Africa, Truth and Reconciliation was not a spectacle; it wasn't entertainment. A writer like Antjie

Opposite: Hlabane township near Boshoek, where three ANC guerrillas were killed in 1985. Their bodies were exhumed by TRC officials, March 1998

Krog, who covered the whole process for South African radio, and who has written an unforgettable book about the experience, was reduced to a walking spectre by what she heard and saw in the hearings.[2] For it was always a question of just how much anyone could stand: the witnesses, the victims, the watching audience. No one who was there was entirely sure that such a bitter catharsis was always a good thing for the country or the individuals to go through. There is an African proverb: Truth is good, but not all truth is good to say.

As Alex Boraine, deputy Chairperson of the TRC, makes clear in his recent memoir, the impetus for the creation of the Commission in 1993 was not just the desire by the majority to unmask apartheid, but also to deal with the legacy of violence in the African National Congress liberation struggle itself.[3] Faced with accusations that it had executed and tortured prisoners in its own training camps in the front-line states of southern Africa, the ANC decided to call for a general inquiry into the past, to include both the apartheid period and the 'liberation struggle'. This double mandate was the crux of the TRC's legitimacy: its task was to assess both the crimes of a regime and the crimes of those engaged in a just war to overthrow it. In the event, neither side in the struggle proved entirely able to face the truth that the TRC uncovered. Both the old regime and the new used the courts to block the Commission's findings. The former State President, F. W. de Klerk, won a court action forcing the Commission to delete findings about his complicity in murders and disappearances. Repentance proved harder to find the higher up the chain of command the Commission went. Most senior figures in the apartheid era regime refused to accept responsibility for torture, killings and other abuses lower down their own chain of command. The ANC government also took the Commission to court to block publication of its indictment of the routine torture of suspected agents and informers in its camps on the South African border and for needless civilian casualties in the armed struggle itself. When faced by the court action of the liberation government that had created the TRC, Desmond Tutu, the Commission Chairperson, famously remarked, 'I have struggled against tyranny. I didn't do that in order to substitute another.'[4] The moral question at issue was whether all is fair in a just war. The Commission's position—that human rights violations remain abuses even when the cause is just—cost it the support of senior figures in the government, including the President, Thabo Mbeki. In the end the court ruled in favour of the Commission and its findings on the ANC were duly published. In view of the resistance its report aroused, it is hard to avoid concluding that the truth the Commission had found remained—and remains—impossible to accept. But this is also to say that it did its job.

There were three phases of the process: first, the victims testified in vast public hearings carried on South African television and radio; then there were amnesty hearings in which perpetrators testified and were cross-examined in order to receive amnesty; finally there were specific sectoral hearings, on the judiciary, business, the media. The process began in 1995, and the amnesty portion of the process was concluded in June 2001.

It was not a general, blanket amnesty for, say, all generals and all top politicians, as had been the case in Chile and Argentina. In South Africa, it was to be a specific amnesty, on a case by case basis, decided by a panel of amnesty commissioners sitting in public hearings. The perpetrators would have to engage in full disclosure, prove that their crimes were political in nature, i.e. connected to an ideological or institutional defence of the regime, and demonstrate that the manner in which the offences were carried out had not displayed sadism or personal gain. Amnesty was not made conditional on repentance. No one had to apologize.

Nothing proved more controversial, inside or outside, than the amnesty provisions of the South African model. For outsiders, the victims' claims to justice were being sacrificed for the sake of conciliating the white power structure. For many insiders, especially victims, the amnesty provisions were asking a society of victims to display a scarcely human forbearance. What outsiders often failed to understand, and insiders knew in their bones, was that the basic reasons for amnesty were political. Amnesty was the precondition for a peaceful transition of power.

I understood the necessity of amnesty when I went to South Africa in 1997 to observe the amnesty hearings myself. The hearings I attended were in the municipal hall in New Brighton, near Port Elizabeth, an industrial city in the Eastern Cape. Every day the perpetrators were brought to the hall in armoured cars, provided by their former colleagues in the local police. They were kept at night in the lock-ups they had once run. When I went into a police station in the Eastern Cape to ask for directions, the entire staff except for one desk sergeant was white. They were still there, behind the barbed wire, behind the high walls of the detention centres. If this was the case in a small provincial police station, I reasoned, the same had to be true of the army and the judiciary. If the whites still held the guns, the police stations, the barracks, a compromise was necessary, between what victims wanted and what the society could stand, between justice and order.

This compromise may have seemed necessary, but the social consensus that sustained it within the majority was thin. The Mxenge family did not agree. Griffiths Mxenge, a heroic anti-apartheid lawyer, had been foully murdered and the family needed justice. You can see this in Jillian Edelstein's photo (p112). I went to see the Mxenge family myself and I can remember the stubborn resentment, the sense of being abandoned by the liberation movement Mxenge had died fighting for. It would be fair to say that amnesty was hell for most victims' families. If so, the reconciliation that follows from amnesty can only be limited, conditional and begrudging. It is best not to sentimentalize South Africa, and best not to sentimentalize reconciliation. Jillian Edelstein's photographs are strong precisely because they sharply constrain the possibilities of sentimentality. They remind us that forgiveness and reconciliation are just words: to have reality they have to become deeds and these deeds must be undertaken by individuals scarred by the past and corroded by mistrust.

A couple of the pictures here bring together one particular story I watched played out in the amnesty hearings in Port Elizabeth. Look at the photograph of Gideon Nieuwoudt together with Mike Barnardo of the witness protection team (p57). Then look at the picture of Joyce Mtimkulu, holding a fistful of her son's hair (p129). Her son, Siphiwo, was a student activist in Port Elizabeth in the 1980s. Nieuwoudt picked him up one night on the streets of Port Elizabeth, drove him out to Post Chalmers (it's also in the book), and together with some other officers, shot him in the back of the head. Then they burned the body on a barbecue. It takes a while to burn a human body, six or seven hours by the policemen's own admission. They drank and talked and turned the body over until the flesh was burned away and all that was left was bones. When these were cold enough to handle, they tossed them into a black garbage bag, threw them in the trunk of the car, and drove to the Fish River. There they threw the remains into the brown waters.

Look again at Joyce's face. Then at Nieuwoudt. For a week in the municipal hall in Port Elizabeth they were barely forty feet apart, she in the front row with 500 people from the shanty towns and small houses of New Brighton behind her, and Nieuwoudt up on stage between protection officers and his lawyers. These lawyers led Nieuwoudt through the story. He was monosyllabic, rarely looked out at the audience gathered there to catch a glimpse of someone whose name had once been a synonym for fear. It wasn't hard to imagine what Nieuwoudt must have been thinking. He had been apartheid's enforcer: the one who slammed people's heads against the radiators in the interrogation rooms in Port Elizabeth police station, the one who understood that fear is what keeps injustice in place. He was one of the lords of the universe, the ones who made sure that five per cent of a country's population enjoyed ninety-five per cent of its wealth; he was the one who gave the others their good life, the safe, walled gardens of privilege, the obedient servants. He was the one who maintained the miracle: a tiny, outnumbered population of whites enjoying paradise undisturbed by danger or conscience.

The people like Nieuwoudt who made the dream possible, however, could not be acknowledged to exist. The State President denied anyone ever slammed people's heads against radiators. The Minister of Justice denied on a stack of Bibles that such things ever went on. So if you are Nieuwoudt, the silence around your daily acts of infamy must be very impressive. You are so important not even your superiors can tell the truth about you. Perhaps they even fear you; not as much, of course, as the people in the townships. But they fear you.

You need to understand all this in order to grasp the meaning of Nieuwoudt's expression as he poses for Jillian Edelstein's remarkable picture. It is remarkable, of course, because of the directness of Nieuwoudt's gaze, the casual male way he holds his cigarette, the hand in his pocket, and above all, the hint of a smile. This man burns people with that cigarette so casually held between the fingers of his right hand. This man seems to enjoy the scrutiny of the camera, hence his own notoriety. The gaze seems to say: Yes, I am apartheid's secret. At the heart of it all, there was me. Without me, we wouldn't have kept paradise to ourselves. You can judge me all you like. I don't care.

Except, of course, that his easy defiance was a contemptible lie. He had actually fought with all his might to stop the hearings, several times taking the Truth Commission to court to prevent disclosure of his name in proceedings, refusing to apply for amnesty, denying all guilt, until the last moment, when he decided that the hearings offered him his best chance of a way out of jail.

In Joyce Mtimkulu Nieuwoudt met his match. She proved to be an implacable foe. She kept her son's hair for twenty years. It fell out when he was poisoned—again on the orders of people like Nieuwoudt, if not Nieuwoudt himself. She kept it in a black plastic bag she took to the hearings so that it could be held up whenever it was needed. It is all she has left of her son besides a few photographs and newspaper clippings. She pursued Nieuwoudt for twenty years—long before the Truth Commission began—and he even came to her house to threaten her, then to torment her by telling her what had happened, then to confess. It was a strange relationship. They could not leave each other alone, this perpetrator and his victim.

She was a formidable woman, much stronger than her shy husband, corrosively sceptical of everything she was told, a shrewd manager of media interest in her son's story, a tough woman who was not fooled.

In one sense she knew the factual truth about her son before the TRC began its work. She knew that he had been 'disappeared'—as they say in Latin America—and that he had been taken to Post Chalmers and killed. What she wanted from the process was for Nieuwoudt to say this truth, out loud, in front of everyone in her community. What she wanted was validation for herself in the form of confession from Nieuwoudt. What she wanted was not knowledge so much as acknowledgement.

I sat beside her as Nieuwoudt and the other officers involved in killing her son told their stories under oath. She did not weep, she just listened, with a kind of ferocious, furious attention. When it was over, she was disgusted. He had not said anything. She believed nothing. Why? I asked. It seemed like a pretty thorough recounting of the story, and he had been cross-examined at length by lawyers representing the family. So what was missing?

He lied about the drugs, she said. Nieuwoudt claimed that before he and his team executed Siphiwo they had woken him up and given him a cup of Nescafé laced with a sleeping pill. It was the little detail of the sleeping pill she couldn't stand. How could a man like Nieuwoudt claim that he had any kind of care for his victim? I was tempted to reply that giving the victim a sleeping pill might only be a management strategy, not a sign of care. But she would have brushed all that aside. The fact was that they were shot like dogs and burned like animals, and that is all the truth there was or ever would be. Sleeping pills! The very idea made her laugh.

You would think, if you were listening to the story of your own son's death, that you wouldn't want every last detail. Joyce made me realize you do want every last detail. And you do not want to be trifled with. You don't want any flannel, any embroidery, any cute little inventions. You want every last detail, as it was. As it really was.

And what does this kind of truth do for a person like Joyce Mtimkulu? It provides official, public acknowledgement, at the highest level, before her own community, with amnesty judges sitting on the dais to confirm its official status. What she wanted was official acknowledgement, validation. She wanted one moment in her life when Nieuwoudt was made to look like a pathetic liar.

Nothing quite like this actually occurred. Everyone wanted the TRC to provide a certain kind of closure: cell doors clanging shut on Nieuwoudt, a large amount of state compensation for Joyce and her family, and a new house and a better TV. But closure happens in the movies, not in real life. In real life, Nieuwoudt got amnesty, Joyce did not get compensation and South Africa remains what it is: a society where a person's chances in life are still determined by the colour of their skin.

Which might imply that the whole TRC process was a waste of time. Worse, it was an exercise in kitsch, in sentimentality, in theatre, in hollow pretence. Not so. Even its harshest critics—those who would charge it was harder on white perpetrators than black ones, that the ANC government escaped serious censure, that Tutu went too far in begging Mrs Mandela for an apology—would concede that something happened in these hearings. What that something was is hard to say. We do not know exactly what the black audience took away at the end of the day. We do not know what the white audiences watching on their television sets made of it all. Many of them, especially those with connections to the security forces, must have dismissed the whole exercise as a kangaroo court.

One could say that the whole process had one irrefutable result. It narrowed the range of impermissible lies that one can tell in public. In Argentina, once the truth of the Videla regime came out, it became impossible not to admit that the regime had taken drugged prisoners and thrown them out of helicopters to drown in the sea. In Czechoslovakia, it became impossible, once lustration commissions had done their work, to deny that large numbers of upstanding Czech citizens had betrayed their neighbours to the secret police. In East Germany, it became impossible to deny that an astonishing percentage of the populace had some connection or other with the Stasi, and that in some cases neighbour had betrayed neighbour, husband betrayed wife, brother betrayed sister and so on.[5] It is sometimes essential that former regimes are shamed into unalterable moral disgrace: that their inner moral essence is named and defined for all time by an objective process of fact-finding. This will foreclose nostalgia and prevent reaction. One central reason, surely, why the democratic transition in Russia has been so difficult is that millions of people continue to be so disabled with nostalgia for the imperial greatness of the Soviet period.[6] Hence they believe that the future lies behind them, in a return to all that hearty brutality and repression. This nostalgia is sustainable only on the basis of systemic lying and the reproduction of impunity for the legions of torturers, guards, executioners, informers and apparatchiks who ran an apparatus of terror that exterminated or incarcerated whole populations for more than thirty years. Any society that allows its torturers to retire with medals and pensions inevitably pays the price. The price of lies is immobilized nostalgia for tyranny. So it is true—and Russia is the proof—that you cannot create a culture of freedom unless you eliminate a specific range of impermissible lies. I put it this way— a range of impermissible lies—because all societies, and all human beings lie to themselves all the time. Citizens of advanced liberal democracies are fooling themselves if they think we live in truth. None of us can support very much truth for very long. But there are a few lies that do such harm that they can poison a society just as there are a few lies in private life that can destroy a life.

Consider the kinds of impermissible lies that the South African Commission had to deal with. In the country clubs and suburban gardens of white South Africa, there must have been many people, by the end of the apartheid regime, who saw the writing on the wall and conceded that the old regime would have to change its ways, even cede power to that nice Mr Mandela. They would have consoled themselves for this recognition by claiming that the system was unsustainable, of course, but not really that bad. A few rotten apples, but those were the exceptions rather than the rule. What the TRC uncovered was something very different indeed: not a few bad apples, not a few bad cops like Gideon Nieuwoudt, but a system, a culture, a way of life that was organized around contempt and violence for other human beings. The truth, the cold core, of apartheid was the Sanlam building in Port Elizabeth where they threw you against radiators and beat you with wet towels. Every South African citizen was contaminated by that degradation, that deadness, that offence against the spirit.

In time to come, when whites are emigrating and there is grumbling in the suburban gardens that the country is going to hell, when they are tempted to say: the old days weren't so bad, just maybe, the words will die in their throats. Because the Truth Commission had rendered some lies about the past simply impossible to repeat.

Likewise, in time to come, when things get hard in South Africa for the ruling majority, they may be tempted to say: We were victims of apartheid. We are the heirs of a just war of national liberation. So all is permitted to us. The laws don't matter. The whites don't matter. Only we matter. Something rather like this may be unfolding in the mindset of the Zimbabwean elite around the embattled President, Robert Mugabe. In this corrupt and criminal elite, the mythology of the liberation struggle against the whites is used to legitimize plunder, illegality and the suppression of democracy. If this can happen in Zimbabwe, there is no particular reason why it cannot happen in South Africa.

Except, of course, that there has been a Truth Commission. As a result of its work, an essential taboo has been broken: the moral legitimacy of the liberation struggle has been subjected to scrutiny, and if the justice of the struggle has been reaffirmed, the crimes committed in the name of the struggle have been identified. It would be an impermissible lie to believe that all is permitted a people who have suffered ultimate injustice. The TRC may have made it impossible to give voice to this lie. As Jillian Edelstein's memorable photographs show, the truth is imperishably lodged in the hearts and minds of those who were there.

1 Ruti G. Teitel *Transitional Justice* (OUP, NY, 2000); Aryeh Neier *War Crimes. Brutality, Genocide, Terror and the Struggle for Justice* (Times Books, NY, 1998); Priscilla B. Hayner *Unspeakable Truths: Confronting State Terror and Atrocity* (Routledge, NY, 2001); Martha Minow *Between Vengeance and Forgiveness* (Beacon Press, Boston, 1998)
2 Antjie Krog *Country of My Skull* (Random House, 1998)
3 Alex Boraine *A Country Unmasked* (OUP, 2001)
4 quoted in Boraine, pp315–316
5 Timothy Garton Ash *The File: A Personal History* (Vintage, 1997)
6 Svetlana Boym *The Future of Nostalgia* (Basic Books, NY, 2001)

Onlookers leaving the site of an exhumation, Vlakplaas, near Pretoria, March 1998

MEMORY AND TRAUMA PUMLA GOBODO-MADIKIZELA

On 21 March 1960 the Pan-Africanist Congress (PAC), a breakaway organization from the ANC established the previous year, held a public protest against the pass laws, the notorious legislation introduced by the apartheid government which required blacks to carry internal passports that regulated almost every aspect of their lives. Several thousand black people gathered outside the police station in Sharpeville, a township in the northern town of Vereeniging. The police opened fire. Sixty-nine people were killed (most of them were shot in the back as they fled and all of them were unarmed) and 186 were wounded. The massacre sparked off countrywide strikes and demonstrations as anger in the black areas mounted. On 30 March the government declared a state of emergency. Twenty thousand people were detained and the PAC and the ANC were banned. The two political organizations were forced underground and some of their members went into exile.

In Langa, one of Cape Town's black townships, where I grew up, the violence was much worse than at Sharpeville. At least this is how I would remember the events I witnessed as a five-year-old child through the hedge in front of our tiny house at 69 Brinton Street. It is a memory that I still find difficult to shake out of my mind. Yet its accuracy was tested when, as a committee member on the Truth and Reconciliation Commission in 1996, I was forced to revisit the events in Langa township not as they lived in my memory, but as they occurred.

What I remembered was the commotion in the row of houses on my street, all replicas of the matchbox-type structure that was my home, linked to each other like carriages in an endless train. Men I knew as the fathers of girls and boys I played with were running around looking scared, jumping fences to be anywhere but in their own homes. Men I had never seen inside my home came out of our coal shed at the back of the house with blackened faces. To escape this chaos of men—scared and defiant men—running in and out of my house, I wandered outside and saw what they were all running from. Big army trucks like huge monsters were roaming the streets, driving over walkways and into the field in front of our house, firing into the fleeing crowds. I was witnessing something I had never seen before: live shooting, blood and death. The image that remained in my memory years later was that of a street covered in blood and bodies lined up like cattle in a slaughterhouse.

This image was recalled with painful clarity on 16 June, 1976 when police opened fire on 10,000 black students in Soweto who were on a peaceful march against the imposition of Afrikaans as the language of instruction. Once again violent protests spread through the townships of Cape Town and the memory of those bodies outside my home in Brinton Street sixteen years before returned me to the site of my childhood. This time I packed my bags and with other students at Forthare University abandoned my studies for the year to join in the protest.

Twenty years after that, in 1996, when I was invited to join the Truth and Reconciliation Commission, I was shocked to learn that what in my memory was a 'massacre' on Brinton Street was not what actually took place. According to the records,

Albertina Sisulu, the wife of ANC leader Walter Sisulu, during his imprisonment, Johannesburg, 1984

confirmed by many of those who organized the 1960s protests, one death resulted from the police shooting in Langa.

What conclusions can be drawn from this serious discrepancy? How can what I remember so vividly turn out to be unconfirmed by reports of what happened on that day? Since the countrywide protest in 1960 was organized by the PAC, I interviewed PAC leaders, including their then president, Clarence Makwethu, more to straighten out what was unresolvable in my mind than to establish the truth for the records of the TRC. But all the evidence suggested that my memory was wrong. Or *was* it? Can what was still so vividly alive in my mind be described simply as a misrepresentation of facts, a reconstruction and exaggeration of events as they happened? What does this tell us about the remembrance of traumatic events?

I can only suggest that when the safe world of a child is shattered by a violent invasion, such as I witnessed in Langa, the intensity of the moment presents itself as something that the world of a five-year-old cannot absorb. The child lacks the psychological capacity to contain the brutality before her eyes and certainly has no language with which to represent the terrible events. Blood, bodies and death are the only meaningful words that capture in images what she cannot articulate in words.

There is a parallel to be drawn here with adult experience. When we are confronted with unimaginable and unbelievable human brutality the effect is to rupture our senses. When the rupture of one's senses is a daily occurrence—as was the case in South Africa's violent political past—old memories fuse with new ones and the accounts given by victims and survivors are not simply about facts. They are primarily about the *impact* of facts on their lives and the continuing trauma in their lives created by past violence. The experience of traumatic memory becomes a touchstone of reality, to borrow a phrase from Maurice Friedman,[1] and tells us more about how people who have survived try to live their normal lives than it does about facts.

Memory renders the account of traumatic events unreliable, so the argument goes. Primo Levi informs us that 'human memory is a marvellous but deceptive tool'.[2] What lies in our memory is not 'engraved in stone' but fades away with time, shifts or swells, incorporating different experiences. This argument has led many to question victims' stories, and to claim that what is remembered amounts to fragments of truth, a *re*construction of past events that fails to rise to the level of truth. Some have even claimed that the memory of traumatic events necessarily involves forgetting[3] which implicitly means that it is unbelievable. While these claims are not unfounded they are nonetheless misleading and ignore the crucial understanding that factual accounts simply tell us very little about how victims continue to live with the memory of terrible events. As we listened over hours, days, weeks and months to the accounts of the victims and survivors who appeared before the TRC, their stories made clear the daily invasion of painful memory into their lives. It seemed that rather than presenting a reconstruction of their past, victims and survivors brought to the public hearings the lived experience of how they remembered it.

It is impossible to describe what it was like listening to these testimonies without being personal about it. Being on the Commission was particularly challenging because most of the victims who appeared before the TRC were black and were women. This

1 Maurice Friedman, 'Why Joseph Campbell's psychologizing of myth precludes the Holocaust as a touchstone of reality', *Journal of the American Academy of Religion,* 66 (1998)
2 Primo Levi, 'The Memory of the Offence', *The Drowned and the Saved* (Vintage NY, Abacus UK)
3 Daniel Abramson, 'Make history not memory: history's critique of memory', *Harvard Design Magazine* (1998)

made their stories real in a very personal way. Being a black woman on the Commission re-exposed me to the multiple meanings of a childhood, student and professional life spent under apartheid in South Africa. I was not a neutral listener. I was not a 'blank screen'.[4] This was true of many of us on the TRC and it was something we had to be careful about. The Commission emphasized even-handedness and any demonstration of emotion was seen as proof of bias. Dealing with other people's memories—which in turn evoke one's own memories—without letting go of one's own emotions was no easy feat. Many of us who served on the TRC continue to struggle with closure; in part because we had to deny our emotions in order to contain the pain of the witnesses before us, and also to ensure the success of a national process everybody was watching.

Contrary to common protestations against revisiting the past, there is an urgency to talk about the past among many of those who have suffered gross violations of human rights. Sometimes retelling a story over and over again provides a way of returning to the original pain and hence a reconnection with the lost loved one. Evoking the pain in the presence of a listening audience means taking a step backwards in order to move forwards. The question is not whether victims will tell their stories, but whether there is an appropriate forum to express their pain. The success of Steven Spielberg's worldwide drive to have survivors of the Holocaust tell their stories, and of Claude Landsmann's *Shoah*, are living examples of the truth of this. But if urgency to recount the past exists, so, too, does its opposite. Some victims and survivors have an ambivalence in the way they approach the past: a strong pull towards forgetting, or rather a denial of memory coexisting with a need to recall the details of the trauma.

With regard to the first I want to tell a story that concerns a seventy-two-year-old woman whose husband was killed in the most brutal of the forced removals of black people in the Western Cape. It happened on Christmas Eve 1976, on what became known as the Black Christmas, a Christmas Day marked with blood, death and a lot of misery. Twenty years later, when she heard on her radio that a truth commission was inviting victims of human rights violations to submit their testimonies, Elsie Gishi could not wait for the formal statement-taking process to begin. She set off immediately for the women's counselling agency in one of the Cape Town townships which had been mentioned as one of the NGOs the Commission would be working with. When I arrived at the agency later that day, Mrs Gishi was sitting on a couch, leaning forward on her walking stick, her eyes focused on the door.

She rushed through the greetings and started to tell me her story. I barely had a chance to take out my notebook and pen. She began with her arrival in Cape Town as a young bride. She told me about her life as a domestic worker in different white homes in the white suburbs of Cape Town, her hard-working husband, the joy of their children, their schooling, and finally the events of that terrible Christmas Eve in 1976. She described her panic as she roamed the streets looking for her children in the midst of wild firing from army trucks. Forced to find shelter she was hit by bullets in her back just as she went into her neighbour's house. Injured, frightened and helpless, she arrived at the hospital where she was chained to her bed and placed under police guard, as was common practice with victims shot by the police in political incidents. While she was in the hospital her neighbours came to tell her that her husband had been found

---

4 'Bearing witness or the vicissitudes of listening', Shoshana Feldman and Dori Laub, *Testimony: Crises of Witnessing in Literature, Psychoanalysis and History* (Routledge, NY, 1998)

dead at home with a deep slash to his head, exposing his brains. This was the signature of the *witdoeke*,[5] the black police collaborators who wreaked murderous havoc on 'Black Christmas'. Mrs Gishi came home from the hospital to find that she had suffered a double loss. Her son had lost his sanity, and here she describes what she perceives to be the cause:

> One of my neighbours told me that my son was in the same van in which my husband was taken to hospital. What my neighbour described to me broke my heart completely … My son … my son Bonisile insisted on accompanying the wounded to the hospital. So he was in the back of the van and saw his father in the worst and most unspeakable state of death any child should see. I was told that he repeatedly asked his dead father, *'Tata, Tata* [Daddy], do you see me, do you see me? Please say yes to me.' He was crying and shaking my husband. On my return from the hospital I found my son's bloodied clothes from throwing himself all over my husband's body … Since then my son has not been his normal self.

It was hard not to be drawn into her story. I saw this little boy's agony, his tears of anguish and utter hopelessness as he stares into the unseeing eyes of death, knowing, but not knowing—'Daddy, please say yes to me'—that his father won't be able to speak to him again. Then I saw this seventy-two-year-old woman, twenty years later, taking her walking stick and braving a thirty-minute walk to the township agency's offices to tell her story to 'someone from the Commission'.

There are several points to notice in this excerpt from Mrs Gishi's testimony. She says that her son found her husband in 'the most unspeakable state of death'. In other words, it was simply *indescribable*. She has no reference point against which to relate her experience. I found that victims often framed their testimonies in language that they themselves confessed was inadequate to describe what they had suffered. And here lies the paradox. Language communicates. At the same time it distances us from the event as it was experienced, limiting our participation in the act of remembering. We cannot fully understand what victims went through because the impact of the event cannot be adequately captured in words. Instead, it is 'lost' in words. So what function does a traumatic narrative serve if it creates a gulf between language and experience? I think it forces us to see that the real story—the *real* story of a violent political past—will be found in the emotional scars carried by thousands of victims and survivors who reflect daily on the destruction visited upon their lives by a brutal political system. This story can never be untrue, because it is the lived experience of what the victim went through. The 'facts' of the experience are marked indelibly on the victim's body and heart and mind.

I would like to contrast the urgency of Mrs Gishi's story with another woman's ambivalence. The Commission frequently held outreach meetings in different communities. In the course of one of these meetings I noticed a woman in the audience sitting defiantly with her back to the stage as my colleague delivered the official TRC message. I understood the meaning of her body language, but I went down the hall to find out why she was so distressed. When I approached her, she turned away from me, then got up and walked out of the hall.

5 'White scarfs', so called because of the white handkerchiefs they wore around their heads to distinguish them from the rest of the people in the township, who were the main target of police.

As she walked she started to speak, first muttering then blurting out, 'Why did you come here? Why did you come here?' It was a brief moment of drama: everyone in the audience turned towards us as I followed her outside. She began to cry and gesturing with her hands said, 'Have you come here to hurt us? Just tell me, have you come here to revive our scars?' She went on tearfully to tell me how she had forgotten, how she had 'put grass over the past', using a Xhosa expression, and moved on. 'And now you want us to remember? Is this going to bring back my son?'

We sat under a tree and I listened to her venting her anger at the Truth Commission, 'a pointless exercise', as she called it, since the TRC was not going to bring her child back. I took her hand and held it between my hands, more to try and take her pain and cleanse myself of the guilt I felt for causing her such anguish, than to comfort her. I asked if I could take her home. As we drove to her house I felt the inadequacy of the word 'sorry' and the frustration of being a messenger who would be here now and gone the next moment, who would not stay to pick up the pieces, but move on to cause more pain. It was an unhappy emotional responsibility.

She invited me into her home—two chairs, a table and a cupboard in the front room and a double bed in the small remaining room of the house. And this is where I saw the unpredictability of testimony as she started to tell her story with vivid detail and with amazing calm:

> My son was eleven years old. He had come home during his school break at ten o'clock. I was sitting right there where you are sitting, just sitting exactly where you are sitting in that chair. He walked in dressed in his school uniform, went to the cupboard over there and opened the drawer to get a knife, and cut himself a slice of bread. He is doing all of this in a rush. He is like that when he comes home during break. He got some peanut butter from the top and spread it on his bread. He put the bread back, but there were crumbs left on the cupboard, and the knife—still smudged with peanut butter. He ran out. He is still chewing his bread and holding it in his hand. It wasn't long—I heard shots outside. Some commotion and shouts. Then I'm hearing, 'uThemba, uThemba, mama ka Themba nanku Themba bamdubule!' [Here is Themba, Themba's mother, they have shot Themba!]. I went flying out of this house. Now I am dazed. I ran, not thinking. My eyes are on the crowd that has gathered—Here is my son, my only child. It was just blood all over. My anguish was beyond anything I ever thought I could experience. They have finished him. I threw myself over him. I can feel the wetness of his blood—I felt his last breath leave him. He was my only child.

This testimony is a compelling example of how witnesses remember the concrete details of the traumatic event: the crumbs left on the cupboard, the knife smudged with peanut butter. It is as if each image is etched in the mother's memory, taking on a new significance in the telling. 'That chair' on which I was sitting, the jar of peanut butter that was always on the cupboard, all these items become symbols of the little boy's 'last act' in his home. Even the crumbs are treasured as a sacred memory. The tenses defy the rules of grammar as they cross and re-cross the boundaries of past and present. 'He *ran* out. He *is* still chewing his bread. … *Now* I am dazed. I *ran* …' The final moment comes when she recalls seeing her son's lifeless body: '*Here is my son*.' With a gesture of her hand she transports the moment from the past into the present, as if the floor in her front room was the place where it all happened, as if her lifeless son's body were lying there at that very moment.

The telling of this story illustrates the tension between remembering and forgetting. One of the questions that arises is whether Mrs Plaatjie was better off before she told her story than she was after telling it. The question can be applied more broadly. We can ask whether remembering benefits societies that have suffered trauma more than forgetting. This is not an easy question to answer, but I think it depends on *how* the past is remembered. If a memory is kept alive in order to kindle and cultivate old hatreds and resentments, then it is likely to culminate in vengeance. But if a memory is kept alive in order to transcend hateful emotions, to free oneself or one's society from the burden of hatred, then remembering has the power to heal.

This may be easier to achieve at an interpersonal level than at the level of societies. Many white South Africans have had to struggle to reconcile their privileged and protected lives with the brutality revealed to the Commission of the system that most of them supported. So they have denied their role in the evil of apartheid and often accused victims of exaggerating. These denials were epitomized by the blatant refusal to admit wrongdoing by many perpetrators of apartheid atrocities, perpetrators who received several promotions under apartheid and who now hold responsible positions under the post-apartheid government.

And this is the problem. Black people are having to deal with the reality that political transformation has not fundamentally transformed their lives, while white people who benefited from apartheid have lost little or nothing. On the contrary, the benefits and luxuries they enjoyed in the past continue today under a black majority government. Very few white people are prepared to face up to this. While their biggest complaint is the rising rate of crime, it is black people who have to deal with the escalating crime in their backyards and inside their homes, as well as coping with the poverty that is the inevitable consequence of years of exclusion under apartheid. Many victims and survivors not only lost their sons and daughters, but lost breadwinners, too. Their stories of loss were recounted again and again as they stood before the TRC.

Most of the victims who testified before the Human Rights Committee were black. But there were also some rare, white witnesses who appeared. One such was a white woman whose son had been killed while serving in the South African Defence Force. Anne-Marie McGregor's son was brought home in a sealed body bag. I approached her after reading about her son's death in the 1987 archives of a community newspaper in the conservative Afrikaans town of Paarl. The conscription of young white South African men is a story that touches every white family in South Africa. We hoped that if Mrs McGregor and others like her would tell their stories in public, then more white people would be able to identify with the transformation that the TRC hoped to achieve. The public hearing in Paarl where Mrs McGregor told her story was reported to have had the largest white audience of all the hearings held by the TRC.

Shortly before I opened the proceedings there, I was handed a typed document with the name of Owen, one of Mrs McGregor's two surviving sons, at the top and a request that it be read at the hearing. What was remarkable about Owen's statement was that he made his dead brother, Wallace, the narrator of the testimony and himself its subject. As I read out the testimony I was overwhelmed by this symbolic act of reversal, giving a dead brother one's own voice and dying in his place.

> My name is Matthew William Wallace McGregor. My brother is dead today and I can think of no good reason why. What did he know about politics? All he knew were the lies. He was told that there were forty thousand Cuban soldiers wanting to invade South Africa, that the blacks of Namibia were communists and wanted to take over South Africa, and that there was a small rebel group called the ANC. My brother did not have time to learn that this was all lies. According to him he died a hero because that's all he knew. I regret that he did not live long enough—my brother— to know the truth ... I want you to know my brother that the people you defended against the ANC all along supported the ANC. The ANC was never a little rebel group. It was the people of South Africa ... I want to ask the National Party if they thought they could get away with these lies. I want them to know that now we all know the truth. To P. W. Botha and his cabinet of those days, why did my brother die? Explain to my mother and my father and to all South Africans how and why my brother died.
> *Why did I die?*
> Regards, Wallace.

This testimony is as much about responsibility for a brother's memory as it is about confronting the leaders of the former apartheid government and asking them: 'What did you do in our name?'

'Why did I die?' asks the dead man from his grave on the public stage of the Truth and Reconciliation Commission. The question is a metaphor for the silence of white people, as if their voices can be heard only through the speech of the dead.

An American friend said after a recent trip to South Africa that it is impossible to find any whites who supported apartheid. This represents the major challenge for racial reconciliation: for a true transformation to take place in South African society, victims, perpetrators and bystanders alike must acknowledge the past. The Truth Commission's public process was an opportunity to examine these complex roles both at individual and collective levels. Victims spoke out at last on the stage of the Commission. Perpetrators faced their shame in public. But many beneficiaries of apartheid privilege have responded to the call to public accountability with silence.

In a public debate on reconciliation which I organized in Cape Town, Mahmood Mamdani, now chair of African Studies at Columbia University, New York, posed a provocative question: 'What I still ask myself is whether it is not easier to live with perpetrators than with beneficiaries.' Reconciliation between victims and perpetrators is not enough. For social transformation to take place, reconciliation has to be between victims and beneficiaries. That is the challenge facing South Africa today.

Hillbrow, Johannesburg,
October 2000

The Truth and Reconciliation Commission's brief was to establish as complete a picture as possible of the causes, nature and extent of gross human rights violations—killings, abductions, torture and 'severe mistreatment'—carried out in South Africa between 1 March 1960 and 10 May 1994, by conducting investigations and holding hearings. It could grant amnesty to any person making a full disclosure about acts carried out to meet a political objective and such deeds had to be proportional to that political objective.

Amnesty stripped victims and survivors of recourse to justice through the courts. To offset this, the Commission had to recommend reparations to restore the human and civil dignity of victims and survivors of abuses. It had to compile a report of its findings and suggest how future human rights violations could be prevented. The radical step of putting truth and reconciliation before justice was justified by the belief that finding out the truth was an overriding priority in establishing a common understanding of the past and using such understanding as a basis to forge a new national identity.

Under the Chairperson, Archbishop Desmond Tutu, and his deputy, Alex Boraine, three committees were set up:

The Human Rights Violations Committee, which had to consider the accounts of victims and survivors through public hearings

The Amnesty Committee, which had to hear amnesty applications. It functioned independently of the TRC and appeals had to be made through the court

The Reparations and Rehabilitation Committee, which had to formulate a policy to assist victims which then would be adopted into South African law.

By December 1995, seventeen commissioners had been appointed. They were chosen from a shortlist of names suggested by political parties, churches and other civil organizations. They included lawyers, human rights activists, religious leaders, academics, politicians, doctors and a psychiatric nurse. The commissioners were: Alex Boraine, Mary Burton, Bongani Finca, Chris de Jager, Sisi Khampepe, Richard Lyster, Wynand Malan, Khozo Mgojo, Hlengiwe Mkhize, Dumisa Ntsebeza, Wendy Orr, Denzil Potgieter, Mapule Ramashala, Fazel Randera, Yasmin Sooka, Glenda Wildschut and Archbishop Tutu. In 1997, a further ten committee members were appointed: Russell Ally, June Crichton, Mdu Dlamini, Virginia Gcabashe, Pumla Gobodo-Madikizela, Ilan Lax, Hugh Lewin, Judith 'Tiny' Maya, Motho Msouhli, Ntsikilelo Sandi and Joyce Seroke.

Overleaf: hearings into the deaths of the Guguletu Seven, Guguletu, Cape Town, February 1997

Archbishop Tutu, who won the Nobel Peace Prize in 1984, was appointed Chairperson of the Truth and Reconciliation Commission by Nelson Mandela in December 1995, with Alex Boraine, a former Progressive Party MP from 1974 to 1986, and founder of the Institute for a Democratic Alternative for South Africa (IDASA), as his deputy. Tutu, who was born in 1931, grew up in Sophiatown, a black township outside Johannesburg, and began his working life as a teacher. In 1957 he resigned in protest at the government's policy of inferior education for blacks and decided to join the Church, which he felt 'could be a good way of serving my people'. He was ordained in 1961 and spent the next fifteen years working in Britain and South Africa for the World Council of Churches. In 1976 he became Bishop of Lesotho and the following year, at the funeral of the black activist Steve Biko, he preached his fundamental belief in the attainment of freedom by peaceful means. He spoke out consistently against apartheid and often used his powers to calm angry crowds, particularly in the increasingly violent confrontations of the 1980s. He became Bishop of Johannesburg and then, in 1986, Archbishop of Cape Town and head of the Anglican Church in South Africa. He retired as Archbishop in 1995. His work at the head of the Truth and Reconciliation Commission was a natural extension of his faith in a peaceful transition to democracy.

Archbishop Desmond Tutu, Chairperson of the Truth Commission, Cape Town, May 1997

Above: **Archbishop Desmond Tutu** Chairperson of the Truth Commission, and his deputy, **Alex Boraine** (left), Cape Town, 1997
Opposite: Two young men from New Brighton township at the Biko amnesty hearings at Centenary Hall, Port Elizabeth, December 1997.
Translations usually went on throughout the hearings in English, Afrikaans, Xhosa, Zulu and other languages and dialects

the mandela united football club

At the end of 1997, Mrs Winnie Madikizela-Mandela appeared at a special hearing of the Truth Commission in Johannesburg to answer allegations about her involvement with the group of men known as the 'Mandela United Football Club'. A number of parents from Soweto had testified about the disappearance of their children after they had come into contact with members of the Football Club. The special investigative unit appointed by the Commission had gathered evidence linking the Club to more than twenty incidents of abduction, assault and murder. The members of the Club, who referred to Mrs Mandela as 'Mommy', testified that they were acting on her orders. In 1988 Stompie Seipei, a fourteen-year-old activist, was kidnapped along with three other teenagers. It was claimed Stompie was a police informer. He was taken back to the Mandela house in Orlando West and beaten by Jerry Richardson, the 'coach' of the Mandela Football Club. His body was found on 6 January 1989. Later the same month Dr Abubaker Asvat, a friend of Winnie Mandela's, who had refused to treat Stompie saying he should be admitted to hospital, was murdered in his surgery. Jerry Richardson was arrested in 1989 for his part in the murders of Stompie Seipei, and two other boys, Lolo Sono and Anthony Tshabala, and in 1990 he was sentenced to death, later commuted to life imprisonment. Thulani Dlamini, also a member of the Mandela Football Club, was sentenced to twenty-five years' imprisonment for the murder of Dr Asvat. In 1997 Richardson was called by the Truth Commission to testify at Mrs Mandela's hearing. He told the commissioners that his orders came from Mrs Mandela and that he reported to her after the murders had been executed. He told the commissioners:

> We started torturing the youths in the manner that the Boers used to torture freedom fighters. The first thing that I did to Stompie was to hold him with both sides, throw him up in the air and let him fall freely on to the ground. And Mommy was sitting and watching us. I think we threw Stompie about seven times in the air and he fell on to the ground. He was tortured so severely that at some stage I could see that he would ultimately die … There was a lot of things that we did to Stompie. We kicked him, we just kicked him like a ball.

Mrs Madikizela-Mandela denied all involvement. She had refused to apply to the Truth Commission for amnesty, believing that she had nothing to answer for. She said: 'I will not apologize for any of my activities under apartheid. I fought and I was part of that struggle to fight for the liberation of the country and I don't owe anybody an apology for that.'

Winnie Madikizela-Mandela conferring with her lawyers, Ismael Semenya (right) and Moses Mavundla, Jiss Hall, Johannesburg, December 1997

On 8 May 1996, at the first hearing of the Truth Commission in Durban, Mrs Joyce Mananki Seipei, the mother of Stompie Seipei, testified about the death of her son. Here she describes how she identified his body:

In 1989 on 30 January, two ministers from Johannesburg Methodist Church arrived ... They told me that they are seeing me in connection with Stompie. They said it was on 29 December in 1988 when Stompie was taken from the Methodist Church together with his friends. They were taken to Mrs Winnie Mandela's house. They said to me they are still searching for Stompie, they don't know whether is he alive or is he dead. And they told me that his friends told them that his brain was leaking. On 13 February 1989 they took me ... to Diepkloof Mortuary. That's where I identified Stompie. His body was decomposed, but your son is your son. I was fighting for my rights. And there were signs that really indicated to me that it was Stompie. After having been killed he was thrown into the river between New Canada and Soweto. You couldn't even identify him. I looked at Stompie because I am his mother. I had a deep look at him. I saw the first sign. I said, 'I know my son. He doesn't have hair at the back.' His eyes were gouged, and I said, 'This is Stompie.' ... He had a scar on his eye. I looked at him at the nose, and he had a birthmark. I looked at his chest and I could see a scar, because he fought with another boy in Tumahole. And I looked at his left hand. It was identical to mine. I looked at his thighs. Stompie was very fit, just like his mother. I looked at his private parts, and my sister just winked her eye. His left leg is similar to mine. Underneath the left leg there was a birthmark as well. And they asked me, 'How much does Stompie weigh?' I said, 'No, the police would know that.' They asked me, 'Was he short or was he tall?' I said, 'He was very short.' But because he had been thrown into the water like a dog that's why he's stretched. They brought his clothes. I said, 'I can see these clothes.' There are two things that I realized as well that indicated to me, that proved to me that it was Stompie. His white hat was there. I looked at his shoes, a new pair of running shoes. I said, 'Yes, they are Stompie's.' I said, 'He used to wear size four.'

Joyce Mananki Seipei, with her daughter whom she calls 'Klein Stompie' (Little Stompie), Johannesburg, December 1997

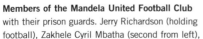

Members of the Mandela United Football Club with their prison guards. Jerry Richardson (holding football), Zakhele Cyril Mbatha (second from left), Charles Slovo Zwame (third from left), Thulani Dlamini (fourth from left), and three prison guards, Niapo (far left), Roberts (far right) and Ntengo (seated), Johannesburg, December 1997

2 December 1997

Jiss Hall (Johannesburg Institute for Social Services),
Mayfair, Johannesburg. Winnie Mandela hearings. Terry
February, one of the press liason officers, has found a
room for me in which to set up a studio. The witnesses,
who are already prison inmates, are housed in the room
behind my studio. It is lunchtime and they are eating
'bunny chow' (large loaves of white bread with the
interior gouged out and replaced with beef or lamb stew
with lots of gristle and potatoes). Terry says he will
bring Mrs Seipei, Stompie's mother, to be photographed.
Just before she arrives, Jerry Richardson, handcuffed and
wearing a strange Barbie badge, appears in my room. He
wants to be photographed with Mrs Seipei. She agrees. A
strange silence accompanies the picture-taking.
Richardson says the small football that he carries is his
good luck charm. When Richardson murdered Stompie Seipei
he was the leader of Winnie Mandela's football club.

Extracted from Jillian Edelstein's diary

Mrs Seipei and **Jerry Richardson**, Johannesburg, 1997

On the last day of the hearings in Johannesburg, Mrs Madikizela-Mandela made a statement in which she alleged that all the witnesses who had testified against her had been lying. In response Archbishop Tutu begged her for an apology.

Archbishop Tutu:

I just want to say we have a very close relationship with the Mandelas. We live in the same street in what is sometimes called 'Beverly Hills'. Our children went to the same schools in Swaziland. They call me uncle. Ms Madikizela-Mandela is godmother to one of our grand-children, who was baptized on the Sunday of Madiba's [Nelson Mandela's] release. When I was Bishop of Lesotho I used to visit Ms Madikizela-Mandela. I have immense admiration for her. There is no question at all that she was a tremendous stalwart of our struggle, an icon of liberation, who was banned, harassed under surveillance, with her husband away serving a life sentence. She was bringing up two young girls. I will never forget her outstanding contribution to the struggle and her indomitable spirit. Everything was done to break that spirit. She was an incredible inspiration to many …

I acknowledge Ms Madikizela-Mandela's role in the history of our struggle. And yet one has to say that something went wrong; horribly, badly wrong … I don't know if we will ever know the details of what went wrong. Many, many love you. Many. Many think you should have been where you ought to be—the first lady of this country. I speak as someone who loves you very deeply, who loves your family very deeply … There are people who want to embrace you … There are many out there who wanted to do so if you were able to bring yourself to say something went wrong. I beg you, I beg you, I beg you, please. I have not made any particular findings on what has happened. I speak as someone who has lived in this community. You are a great person, but you don't know how your greatness would be enhanced if you would say: 'Sorry, things went wrong.'

Winnie Madikizela-Mandela:

Thank you very much for your wonderful wise words, and that is the father I've always known in you. I will take this opportunity to say to the family of Dr Asvat how deeply sorry I am, and to say to Stompie's mother how deeply sorry I am.

It is true, things went horribly wrong. For that part of those painful years when things went horribly wrong, and we were aware that there were factors that led to that, for that I am deeply sorry.

Winnie Madikizela-Mandela, Johannesburg, December 1997

The former John Vorster
Square, where detainees and
prisoners of the Security Police
were held, now Johannesburg
Central Police Station, 2000

Steve Biko's only crime was ignoring his banning orders. His nightmare began when they chained him naked to a wall . . .

the death of steve biko

Steve Biko, the leader of the Black Consciousness movement, died in Pretoria on 12 September 1977. He was beaten into a coma during interrogation by security officers in the Eastern Cape city of Port Elizabeth and then driven, manacled and naked in the back of a police Land-Rover, over 700 miles to Pretoria. The inquest found that Biko had died of head injuries inflicted over a period of several days during his detention by the security police. In January 1997 five security policemen came forward to confess to the assault that led to Biko's death. One of the five, Gideon Nieuwoudt, was among the most feared security policemen in the Eastern Cape. His application for amnesty was successfully opposed by the Biko family— Biko's widow, Ntsiki, his two sons, Samora and Nkosinathi, and his sister Nbandile Mvovo.

Amnesty hearings, Port Elizabeth, Eastern Cape, December 1997

31 March 1998

My son Gabriel and my friend Laura have come to visit me at the amnesty hearings in Cape Town. They find me downstairs photographing Gideon Nieuwoudt, the applicant and perpetrator. He asks me whether I would like to join him and his witness protector for a drink tonight in a bar in Belville (the conservative northern suburbs of Cape Town). I say I can't.

Gideon Johannes Nieuwoudt (left) and Mike Barnardo, a member of the witness protection team, Cape Town, 31 March 1998

Ntsiki Biko, the widow of Steve Biko, Port Elizabeth, 1997

We go to find Steve Biko's elder brother, Khaya. It is late and dark. A bright central light illuminates every block of, say, ten or fifteen houses, a feature which repeats itself over endless rows. In Soweto these lights are called 'Apollos'. George Luse, my fixer, says these high mast lights were 'the eyes of the state' in security terms through the Seventies and Eighties. I've always found it impossible whenever I've seen them not to think of a concentration camp.

Belgium Biko, the younger brother of Steve Biko, at the Biko family home, Ginsburg location, King William's Town, February 1997

robben island

31 December 1997

When I made this my first trip to the Island it was with mixed emotions—one of which was guilt, a common White South African theme. For years as a little girl growing up in White suburban Cape Town, I would look forward to Friday nights when we used to have dinner in Sea Point with my grandparents. From their balcony I would stare across the expanse of ocean all the way to Robben Island, a dark dot on the horizon. My earliest political memory is of my parents hiding Gertie, my black nanny, and her boyfriend, Ben, while the police were raiding homes searching for 'illegal' migrant workers—those who were not carrying their passes, the document which the Blacks referred to as 'the dompas'. These were the result of an inhuman piece of legislation designed to keep tabs on the movements of the black populace all the time. An early photograph shows me snug and secure smiling as I straddle Gertie's chunky shoulders. I adored her and the fear of that raid and the thought that Gertie might disappear from my life began to make me understand a little of what politics was about. I certainly knew that Mandela was imprisoned on the Island but at that time—I must have been about five or six years old—my concerns were centred on the Cadbury's chocolate slab my grandfather used to give us children every Friday night.

Nelson Mandela was held here as a political prisoner by the South African government for a brief term in 1962, and for eighteen years between 1964 and 1982, after which he spent the next six years in Pollsmoor Prison and two in Victor Verster prison, outside Cape Town. He was released on 11 February 1990. The prison at Robben Island was referred to as 'The University' because of the instruction political prisoners received there from their fellow inmates. Interned alongside Mandela were some of the leading members of the anti-apartheid movement including Robert Sobukwe, the founder of the Pan-Africanist Congress (a breakaway group whose members objected to the ANC's Freedom Charter because it included Whites, Coloureds and Asians) and Ahmed Kathrada, the Indian anti-apartheid leader, who had worked alongside Mandela and the ANC since the early 1950s.

Robben Island is known for its extreme temperatures. It has very cold winters and blazing summers from which there is little natural shelter. A watchtower overlooks the bleak courtyard where the inmates took breaks during the day. Robert Sobukwe was held in isolation on a small plot near the watchtower for over twenty years. A single ferry, the *Susan Kruger* (named after the wife of Jimmy Kruger, the Minister of Justice in the National Party who became Minister of Prisons in 1974), transported prisoners and visitors to and from the island during the apartheid years. It was only in late 1997 that the first black-owned company launched its own ferry. On its maiden voyage it carried Ahmed Kathrada, now head of the Robben Island Museum Council, back to the island. Today the tour guides who shepherd tourists around the island are often young men who were imprisoned there themselves during apartheid.

Robben Island prison, 31 December 1997

The courtyard, Robben Island, 1997

Area for non-contact visits, Robben
Island, 1997

Communal dormitory,
Robben Island, 1997

'I was assigned a cell at the head of the corridor. It overlooked the courtyard and had a small eye-level window. I could walk the length of my cell in three paces. When I lay down, I could feel the wall with my feet and my head grazed the concrete at the other side. The width was about six feet, and the walls were at least two feet thick. Each cell had a white card posted outside it with our name and our prison number. Mine read, 'N. Mandela 466/64', which meant I was the 466th prisoner admitted to the island in 1964. I was forty-six years old, a political prisoner with a life sentence, and that small cramped space was to be my home for I knew not how long.'

From *Long Walk to Freedom* by Nelson Mandela (Little, Brown)

Nelson Mandela's cell, Robben Island, 1997

Nelson Mandela was born in 1918 in Mvezo, a village in the Transkei 800 miles east of Cape Town. His great-grandfather was Ngubengcuka, king of the Thembu, part of the Xhosa nation, and Mandela is often called by his clan name 'Madiba'. He trained as a barrister and set up a practice with Oliver Tambo, who later headed the ANC in exile during Mandela's imprisonment. In 1956 Mandela was one of 156 black activists charged with treason and prosecuted by the South African government. In March 1961 they were found not guilty. The ANC and the PAC had been banned the previous year, after the Sharpeville massacre had sparked off countrywide demonstrations, and Mandela went underground to continue his work. From his hideouts, one of which was Lilliesleaf Farm in Rivonia just outside Pretoria, he organized a national three-day workers' strike or 'stay at home' beginning on 29 May. The government retaliated by banning all meetings, conducting household searches and office raids and passing a law which allowed them to detain people without trial. It was clear to Mandela and his comrades that peaceful resistance was useless. In June 1961 Umkhonto we Sizwe (the Spear of the Nation), the military wing of the ANC, was formed. Its high command included Joe Slovo, the head of the South African Communist Party, Walter Sisulu, and Mandela himself. On 5 August 1962 Mandela was arrested again, charged with leaving the country without proper papers and with organizing the strike. He was sentenced to five years' imprisonment and transferred to Robben Island. Weeks later the police raided Lilliesleaf Farm and discovered documents relating to planned guerrilla operations. Mandela was brought back from Robben Island charged with sabotage and conspiracy. At the end of his defence, Mandela made a statement which concluded with the following words: 'During my lifetime, I have dedicated myself to this struggle of the African people. I have fought against white domination and I have fought against black domination. I have cherished the ideal of a democratic and free society in which all persons live together in harmony and with equal opportunities. It is an ideal which I hope to live for and to achieve. But if needs be, it is an ideal for which I am prepared to die.' He was released from imprisonment in February 1990.

6 February 1997

I am to meet Anthony Lewis of the New York Times
Magazine at Tuynhuys, the Presidential house, at 8 a.m.
I have ten minutes to photograph Mandela. I am not to
use flash under any circumstances. Working in the
limestone quarry on Robben Island has damaged the
retinas of the President's eyes.

President Nelson Mandela, Cape Town, 1997

The road between Cradock and Post
Chalmers, Eastern Cape, February 1997

the cradock four

Cradock is a small farming town in the Eastern Cape about 300 miles north of Port Elizabeth. Michausdal and Lingelihle, its two black townships, have a long history of resistance to apartheid. At the beginning of the 1980s Matthew Goniwe, the head of Lingelihle Secondary School, was asked by ANC representatives to organize resistance in the Cradock area. In early 1985 he became a regional executive of the United Democratic Front (UDF) and his role extended to the whole of the Eastern Cape. On 27 June 1985 Goniwe and three other comrades, Fort Calata, Sparrow Mkonto and Sicelo Mhlauli, set off to a political meeting in Port Elizabeth. They never returned. Their mutilated bodies were found a week later. Their funeral was the catalyst for the declaration of a partial State of Emergency in the Eastern Cape. Two of their widows, Sindiswa Mkonto and Nomonde Calata, still live in Cradock. In April 1996 Nomonde Calata described to the Truth Commission how she and Nyami had waited for news of their husbands the day after they disappeared:

> We were unhappy and we slept on Friday without knowing what had happened to our husbands ... Some friends said I must go to Nyami. Nyami was always there for me and I was only twenty at the time and I couldn't handle this ... And when I got there Nyami was crying terribly ... it affected me also ... [The TRC transcript noted that Nomonde was crying loudly while the interpreter finished.]

She went on to describe the moment she realized her husband might be dead.

> Usually *The Herald* was delivered at home ... I looked at the headlines, and one of the children said that he could see that his father's car was shown in the paper as being burned. At that moment I was trembling because I was afraid of what might have happened to my husband, because I wondered, If his car was burned like this, what might have happened to him?

In January 1997, six members of the Port Elizabeth security police applied for amnesty for the killing of the Cradock Four. It was refused.

Nombuyiselo Mhlauli (left) and **Nyami Goniwe**, Cape Town, 4 April 1998

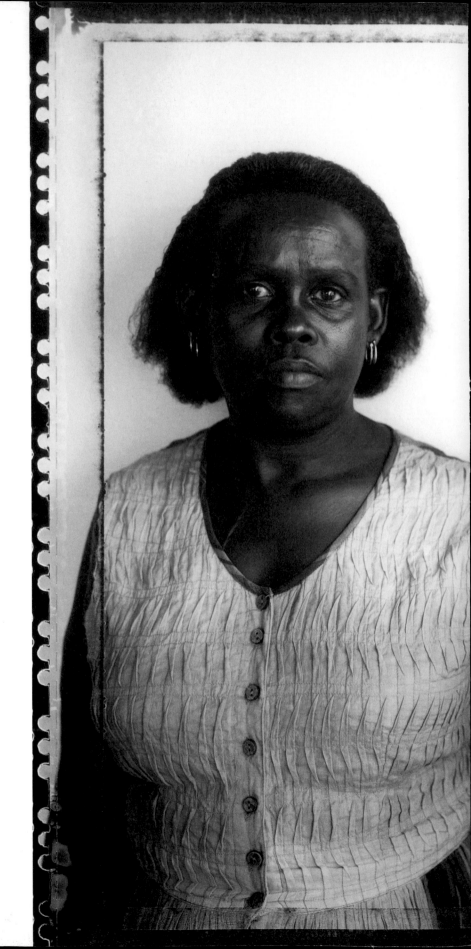

Sindiswa Mkonto and
Nomonde Calata, widows of two of
the Cradock Four, Michausdal
township, Cradock, February 1997

11 February 1997

Nomonde Calata drives with me and George Luse to Post
Chalmers. Her pain is palpable. George tells me both
Nomonde and Mrs Mkonto have suffered terrible trauma and
depression since their husbands' deaths. The sky is dark
and threatening. The road feels endless, punctuated only by
the odd horror story, 'Oh, this is where the remains of the
Pebco Three were found, in that river, there.' The silence
is eerie. It seems as if everything has come flooding back
for Nomonde. She is close to tears and quiet.

Sindiswa Mkonto and her son, **Lonwabo**, in Lingelihle township
where she lived with her husband, Sparrow, February 1997

Memorial to the Cradock Four,
Cradock, Eastern Cape, 1997

Lizzie James came forward to give evidence at the TRC hearings in Cradock about the death of her son, Rocky. He was killed in November 1977 after joining a student boycott in Cradock to protest at being taught in Afrikaans at school. According to Mrs James's statement, the municipal police arrived at her house in the evening saying they wanted to arrest Rocky because of his involvement in the school boycotts. One of the police was heard to say that he would 'tame him for good'. The police took Rocky to the Black Local Authority offices where he was kept for the night. The next day Mrs James heard that her son had been shot whilst trying to escape. Later she learned that a number of pupils had been arrested and beaten throughout the night. In the morning one of the policemen opened the door and told her son to flee. When he turned and ran he was shot in the back and killed. At the end of the TRC document which victims filled in before the hearings was a section headed 'Expectations and Consequences'. Lizzie James's entry read: 'I am expecting to be paid money for the loss of my son.'

Lizzie James, Cradock, February 1997

Eunice Nombulelo Ngubo came forward to give evidence about the death of her brother, Mzwandile Wellington Ngubo. After he had been accused of being a police informer, students in Cradock township set upon the family home and burned it to the ground. This happened on two occasions, once in 1977 and then again in October 1985. She told the Commission that her mother had died as a result of hearing about the loss of her home, and described the day the house had been attacked and burned down.

> A little while after Wellington had arrived, Vincent then came, my younger brother. He then asked for Wellington, because he said there are people here who have come to burn him. I then warned him to hide. When I looked through the window there was a whole horde of people. He then ran away to our next door neighbours. Then a whole lot of children asked for my brother. I said he is here. They started burning down the house, throwing everything around. There were three babies crawling in the house and others, too. I forgot the children. Meanwhile the older children had taken the crawling ones. The little girl crawled towards the fire, then I helped another little girl to go through the window to take out the little baby. I then became unconscious.

She went on:

> The reason why I came before the Commission is because we do not have a home. We stay in shacks. If the Commission could build us a house, please.

Eunice Nombulelo Ngubo, Cradock, 10 February 1997
Overleaf: the Human Rights hearings in Cradock, February 1997

comforters

The Truth Commission employed professional 'comforters' at the hearings whose job it was to look after those who came to testify, both victims and perpetrators. They were to support them before and after their testimonies. When victims were overcome with emotion because of the stories they were telling, the comforters would use human contact to support them—stroking them, holding them, providing them with tissues to dry their tears and glasses of water to help them recover. Pumla Ndulula had worked for three years as a Truth Commission comforter in Johannesburg and in Pretoria. When asked what her 'big cases' had been, she said that she had 'looked after' Colonel Eugene de Kock, the security commander at Vlakplaas who became known as 'Prime Evil'.

Pumla Ndulula, Jiss Hall, Johannesburg, 23 October 1999

Fikile Mlotshwa, a comforter for hearings in the Johannesburg area, 29 May 1997

Nocawe Mafu had been employed as a comforter and briefer in the Eastern Cape region from the start of the Truth Commission hearings. After graduating from high school, she took a nursing degree and qualified as a general nurse, midwife and psychiatric nurse. She has always been involved in human rights organizations, especially those dealing with women's rights. When asked about her role at the TRC hearings, she said, 'It is to smooth their [the victims'] path. It [testifying] is not easy to do. They repress what happened in the past. It is painful, stressful, traumatic. My emotions must not supersede the victim's. I have to be strong for the victim.' She is seen here holding the hands of Mrs Nomonde Calata, one of the widows of the Cradock Four.

Nocawe Mafu, Cradock, 10 February 1997

Vlakplaas, March 1998

Vlakplaas

Vlakplaas was the farm near Pretoria which from the late 1970s served as the base for a special counter-insurgency section of the South African Police. The section was made up of trained 'askaris'—black activists who had been 'turned' to work with the white security forces—who were divided into active units under police command. The units at Vlakplaas were ostensibly set up to maintain law and order, but their members were trained to torture and to kill. Similar units were also set up in Kwazulu/Natal and in the Eastern Cape. Between 1983 and 1993 Vlakplaas operatives were responsible for undercover operations which included the infiltration of ANC organizations and the abduction, torture and murder of thousands of anti-apartheid activists. The bodies of their victims were buried secretly, burned or dumped in the nearby Hennops River. Two of the most infamous commanders at Vlakplaas were Captain Dirk Coetzee (1980–81) and Colonel Eugene de Kock (1985–1993). Also working with the commanders at Vlakplaas was Joe Mamasela, a former ANC undercover agent who had begun to work with the security police in 1981 and was involved in some of the most brutal Vlakplaas operations.

In his book investigating the Vlakplaas death squads[1], the South African journalist Jacques Pauw writes: 'What distinguished the squad's members from common criminals was that they believed themselves to be fighting a secret twilight war against an evil enemy. Any method that could lead to the destruction and disruption of the enemy was permitted and tacitly condoned...' Pauw also describes the euphemisms commonly used for words such as murder and assassinate: *vat hom uit* (take him out), *raak ontsle van hom* (get rid of him), *los die problem op* (solve the problem) and the favourite: *elimineer* (eliminate).

Coetzee, de Kock and Mamasela gave evidence to the Truth Commission describing the murders they had ordered or committed. Mamasela refused to apply for amnesty, saying he had been a victim of the white security forces, but agreed to co-operate with the Truth Commission and gave evidence behind closed doors.

Coetzee and de Kock, when making their statements to the Truth Commission, refused to take responsibility for their actions, saying they had been obeying orders from senior officers in the South African Police, government ministers, the State Security Council and even the President. Because the existence of covert organizations within the South African Police and the South African Defence Force was never publicly acknowledged, when questioned, most of these senior offices and ministers either refused to come forward or denied all knowledge of what had gone on. The farm at Vlakplaas is now occupied by an Afrikaner family. The cells for detention and interrogation have been converted into children's bedrooms.

The former headquarters of the Vlakplaas counter-insurgency unit, March 1998

1 *Into the Heart of Darkness* (Jonathan Ball, Johannesburg, 1997)

Inside Vlakplaas, March 1998

Children playing by the Hennops River, Vlakplaas 1998

Five perpetrators
From left: Warrant Officer Paul van
Vuuren, Brigadier Jack Cronje
(commander at Vlakplaas 1983–85),
Colonel Roelf Venter, Captain Wouter
Mentz and Captain Jacques Hechter,
Amnesty hearings, Pretoria,
February 1997

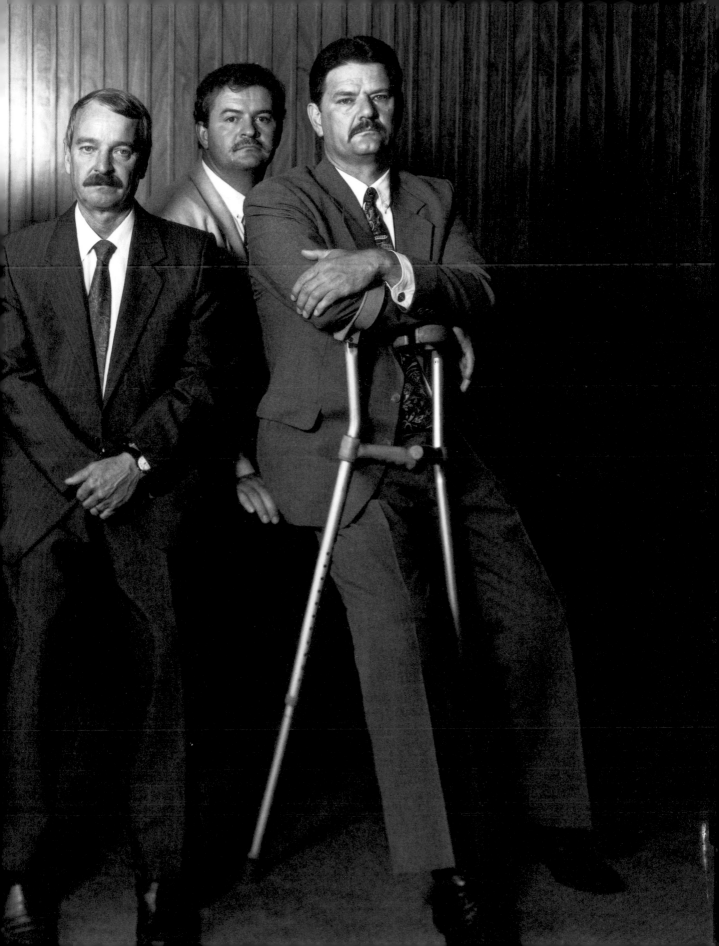

In February 1997 five members of the security police, Paul van Vuuren, Jack Cronje, Roelf Venter, Wouter Mentz and Jacques Hechter, appeared before the Truth Commission in Pretoria. They were applying for amnesty for more than forty murders between them, as well as for incidents of bombing and torture. In their opening statement they said they had decided to come forward 'with a purpose of cleansing our souls from the darkness of the past and to let the truth be spoken about our deeds'. In 1987 Van Vuuren, Hechter and Cronje, together with Joe Mamasela, a black askari serving at Vlakplaas, strangled, suffocated and shot a suspected ANC member, Richard Motasi, and then killed his wife, Irene. They fled the house, leaving the murdered couple's six-year-old son, Tshidiso, alone overnight with the bodies. At the hearings in Pretoria Captain Jacques Hechter described the attack:

> We got out a distance from the house. We were wearing dark clothes and balaclavas. Mamasela's wasn't over his face, just rolled down low. He knocked on the Motasis' door and asked if Richard was in … When Mamasela told us that Richard's wife was expecting him, we decided to wait for him inside. Mamasela knocked on the door again. When the woman opened the door, Mamasela pushed her with a gun to a back room, where he had to keep her from seeing us. We switched off the lights but left the television on so that it seemed that someone was there. We then hid behind the couch. Then a vehicle arrived: his Mazda. He came to the door and found it locked. He was struggling with the lock when we jerked him inside … He struggled violently—he fought like a tiger—and he shouted wildly. To bring him under control I started to strangle him and Van Vuuren smothered him with a pillow over his face. He then fired four shots with his AK-47—the pillow was the silencer … then we called Mamasela, 'Come on, we're finished.'

Van Vuuren then described the death of Irene Motasi:

> I went to the room … if I remember correctly, the woman's head was under the blanket or the sheet, but her head was covered. I told Mamasela, 'You must come, we are finished.' And then I turned around and ran out. Heard shots. When I got outside, Mamasela was next to me. I said, 'What did you do?' He told me that he shot the woman also because she saw his face. I just want to mention that at that time it was not strange that people would recognize Mamasela … He told me that he was going to get plastic surgery at the state's expense.

In a later interview, Mamasela claimed it was Hechter who had shot Irene Motasi, and Hechter who had ordered him to kill their son. Mamasela said: 'I saw this innocent little thing and his face mirrored the face of my child and I just couldn't do it.'

Tshidiso Motasi, the son of Richard and Irene Motasi, Dlangamandla Street, Soweto, September 1998

I follow Dirk Coetzee's detailed instructions down
jacaranda-lined Isipingo Street. For a few short weeks
every year, this dull brown town is turned purple by a
mass of exquisite blossom. My first impression is of how
heavily Coetzee has incarcerated himself. His Rottweilers
are snarling, and the barbed wire around the metal gates
glistens in the sunshine. Tea is served in china cups on
a floral tray. So civilized, I think, holding my cup and
saucer. I notice that wherever Coetzee goes, the leather
purse which hangs off his wrist like a little handbag
goes with him. 'It contains my gun,' he informs me.
'I take it everywhere, even when I go to the toilet.'

Dirk Coetzee was the first commander of the special 'counter-insurgency' unit at Vlakplaas. He had ordered the deaths of many ANC activists, including Griffiths Mxenge, a human rights lawyer, who was stabbed forty times at Umlazi Stadium in Durban, and Sizwe Kondile, a young law graduate from the Eastern Cape, who was interrogated and beaten then handed over to Coetzee who had him shot and his body burned. Coetzee's career at Vlakplaas was short-lived. He was demoted first to the narcotics division and then to the flying squad and in 1986 was discharged from the police force. In 1989, prompted by the last-minute confession about the unit at Vlakplaas by one of Coetzee's colleagues, Almond Nofomela, who was attempting to avoid execution on death row for a non-political murder, Coetzee exposed the undercover operations of the SAP in an interview with the journalist Jacques Pauw. For the next three years, Coetzee lived in exile. He returned to South Africa in 1993, and in May 1997 was tried and found guilty for his role in the murder of Griffiths Mxenge. But he had applied to the Truth Commission for amnesty and in August 1997 he was granted amnesty for Mxenge's murder. At the TRC hearing in Durban, Coetzee was asked what he felt about what he had done to the Mxenge family. He said he felt:

> … humiliation, embarrassment and the hopelessness of a pathetic, 'I am
> sorry for what I have done' … What else can I offer them? A pathetic
> nothing, so in all honesty I don't expect the Mxenge family to forgive
> me, because I don't know how I ever in my life would be able to forgive
> a man like Dirk Coetzee if he'd done to me what I've done to them.

Dirk Coetzee, Pretoria, 26 February 1997

Griffiths Mxenge, a popular forty-six-year-old ANC civil rights lawyer, was found stabbed to death in a cycle stadium in Umlazi, Natal, in November 1981. Four years later his wife, Victoria, also a lawyer, was shot and axed to death at her home in front of her children. In 1989, Dirk Coetzee confessed to organizing Griffiths Mxenge's murder on the orders of Brigadier van der Hoven, the regional security police commander in Port Natal. At an amnesty hearing in Durban in 1996, Coetzee described the setting up of the murder.

> From early November onwards we were operating as a whole
> Vlakplaas team ... and as usual I reported to Brigadier van der Hoven's
> office as officer commanding ... for debriefing and briefing. A few days
> before 19 November [the day of the murder], he asked me to make a
> plan with Mr Mxenge. He then in very short terms briefed me that
> [Mxenge] was an ex-Robben Island convict, that he was an attorney,
> that they were trying to build up a case against him because he was an
> acting instructing attorney in the cases of all ANC cadres who were
> caught in the country, and ... [van der Hofen] said we must not use
> guns or make him disappear, we must make it look like a robbery.

Coetzee's team included David Tshikalanga, Almond Nofomela, Joe Mamasela and Brian Ngqulunga. Tshikalanga was also questioned about the attack:

> Marais [Tshikalanga's legal representative]: Mr Tshikalanga, the body of
> Mr Mxenge had a great number of stab wounds when it was discovered.
> If I am not mistaken, it was in the region of forty. Why was it necessary
> ... to inflict that many wounds?
> Tshikalanga: If I am telling the truth ... it is because he was fighting for
> himself ... it's then that we were forced to stab him so ... He was not
> just offering himself as a sacrifice, but he was refusing when he had the
> pains. He tried to defend himself. Even by hands and all, he was trying
> to fight ...

Coetzee, Tshikalanga and Nofomela were convicted of Griffiths Mxenge's murder in May 1997, but in August 1997 they were granted amnesty by the Truth Commission. The TRC said that there was no doubt that Coetzee had acted 'on the advice, command or order of one or more senior members of the Security Branch' and that all four men had carried out the killing 'because they regarded it as their duty as policemen ... engaged in the struggle against the ANC and other liberation movements ...' The Mxenge family opposed Coetzee's application for amnesty. Mhlele Mxenge, Griffiths Mxenge's brother, said, 'My main objection is that amnesty promotes the interests of the perpetrators, as once they are granted amnesty they are not criminally liable and no civil action can be instituted against [them], and that is totally against the interests of the victims. It is totally unjust.'

Mhlele Mxenge with a portrait of his brother Griffiths Mxenge and Victoria Mxenge, Bisho township, King William's Town, May 1997

11 February 1997

Butterworth is like any other township, except it is situated in the Transkei, puppet state (or homeland) of the former nationalist government. Charity Kondile is smartly dressed in a starched white skirt and jacket. The outfit is Hollywood but the matchbox-sized house with its corrugated iron roof is not. She rages about Dirk Coetzee and his bragging about the murder of her son. When faced with her presence at his amnesty hearing, Coetzee said: 'I did not have the courage to look her in the face.'

Charity Kondile's son, Sizwe Kondile, a newly graduated law student, ANC activist and new father, was murdered in 1981 on the orders of Dirk Coetzee. She had spent nine years trying to find out what had happened to her son. In April 1996 she attended the TRC Human Rights hearings in East London where she explained what she knew about the circumstances of his death. Then, in November 1996, she attended the Amnesty hearings in Durban where in Coetzee's presence she heard how her son had been detained illegally and held by the police security in Jeffrey's Bay police station in the Eastern Cape. There he sustained head injuries during interrogation by the police. According to Coetzee, the police had been scared they might have a 'second Biko' case on their hands, and he and his squad had been called in to 'dispose of' Kondile. Kondile was taken to Komatipoort, on the Mozambique border, where Coetzee and a group of security officers first poisoned him, then shot him, after which they disposed of the body. Coetzee testified:

> The four junior non-commissioned officers ... each grabbed a hand and a foot, put it on to the pyre of tyres and wood, poured petrol on it and set it alight. Now ... the burning of a body to ashes takes about seven hours, and whilst that happened we were drinking and even having a *braai* [barbecue] next to the fire. Now, I don't say that to show our braveness, I just tell it to the Commission to show our callousness and to what extremes we have gone in those days ... the chunks of meat and especially the buttocks and the upper part of the legs had to be turned frequently during the night to make sure that everything burned to ashes. And the next morning, after raking through the rubble to make sure that there were no pieces of meat or bone left at all, we departed and all went on our own way.

Charity Kondile, Msobomvu township, Butterworth, Transkei, February 1997

Post Chalmers, near Cradock,
Eastern Cape, 1997

Post Chalmers is a disused and desolate police station off the national road some twenty miles from Cradock. A convenient rural jailhouse. The sign which announces Post Chalmers as a Holiday Farm is the first untruth. Barbed wire runs the course of the property which is scattered with African thorn trees. It was here that brutal tortures and murders took place. The Pebco Three and Siphiwo Mtimkulu among others were detained here and the police came and went as they pleased during what were often illegal incarcerations. Another lie would be to suggest that anyone held here had a chance of leaving with their lives.

On 8 May 1985 Qwaqwahuli Godolozi, Sipho Hashe and Champion Galela, leaders of the Port Elizabeth Civic Organization (Pebco), a group responsible for mobilizing anti-apartheid activists in the Eastern Cape, disappeared on their way to the airport. They had been fooled into believing they were to meet a British diplomat to discuss funding from abroad. In fact, the meeting had been set up by white security policemen to lure them into a trap. The three men, who later became known as the Pebco Three, were taken to Post Chalmers, the isolated police station near Cradock, where they were interrogated and gradually beaten to death. The black askari Joe Mamasela, who became a state witness in the mid-1990s in return for police protection, was also involved in the abduction. He described how the three men were put into an 'animal shed' at Post Chalmers, where they were interrogated. He said:

> It was brutal. They were tortured severely. They were brutalized. I strangled them. They were beaten with iron pipes on their heads, kicked and punched. They were killed, they died one by one. I have never seen anything like it in my life. It was blazing hell on earth.

Cells where activists were detained, interrogated and tortured, Post Chalmers, 1997

In April 1996, the widows of the Pebco Three testified at the Human Rights hearings of the Truth Commission in East London. Mrs Galela described what had happened on the day her husband disappeared.

On 8 May my husband came home with Mr Hashe from their offices and he was carrying food so that I can prepare it for him, and he told me that they have to rush to the airport for the British Consulate, but he wants to eat first. And I told him that I was busy preparing food and it was winter, a bit dark. I said to my husband, 'Shall we eat when you come back? You know that the councillors want you every time.' I took a very black hat and put it on his head, after a minute the yellow van [arrived] driven by Mr Hashe who was already wearing a hat … They went off then to go to the airport … When they left for the airport it became dusk and they didn't come back.

Lehlohonolo Galela, the son of Champion Galela, one of the Pebco Three, New Brighton township, 13 February 1997

When I visited Mrs Hashe she had a gaping hole in the
roof of her house covered with black plastic sacks. It had
been like that since 1985. She spoke of her relief at
finally knowing what had happened to her husband and how
he had died. 'I saw the Hennops River [near Cradock] where
they put the ashes of the Pebco Three.'

Mrs Hashe's husband, Sipho Hashe, had already spent ten years imprisoned on Robben Island between 1963 and 1973 for his ANC activities. The Hashe house had been petrol bombed both before and after his disappearance as one of the Pebco Three in 1985. Like the other widows, Mrs Hashe waited fifteen years to find out what had happened to her husband. She attended the Truth Commission Human Rights hearings in Port Elizabeth in February 1997, where she described her husband's first arrest at the hands of the security forces:

> My husband woke up and went to open the door. When he asked who they were, they said they were police. And then they came in. They just said, 'Put on your clothes, we have arrived.' … At the back there were some people in the shadow and this person came forward and asked, 'Is it Hashe?' and then when we affirmed that it was him, they said he must just put on his clothes and then he must go … And during this period when they came to arrest him, they were kicking everything in the house and there was something which had a sentimental value, my sewing machine which I got, which my husband bought for me when I attended school. They broke this machine to which I was so sentimentally attached and they took my husband away.

Ten years later, after Mrs Hashe had been repeatedly harassed by the security police as she struggled to make a living selling vegetables, a car drew up at her door:

> I got into the house … and prepared the children for bed. I went out just a few minutes, there was a car. I was wondering what car it was. And they asked me if I knew the man in the back of the van after ten years. I said, 'Yes, he's my husband.' I was now at my house number 21 … he went out [of the van], two Xhosa security men went with him into the house. The first thing he asked me, 'Do you still accept me, because I will never leave fighting for the freedom of the people?' I said, 'Yes, why not?' Then we laughed and went into the house. While we were busy sitting, these police gave him documents—a banning order.

Mrs Elizabeth Hashe, the widow of Sipho Hashe, KwaZakele, New Brighton township, Port Elizabeth, February 1997

Papama was five years old and her brother, Mkhonto Sizwe, one year old, when their father disappeared in 1985. For fifteen years they had no idea what had happened to him. When I asked Mrs Godolozi what she felt about the role of the TRC in bringing the fate of her husband to light, she said, 'I did not have a chance to talk before. It was inside. It was painful inside. I still do not believe the security police—they keep changing their story. I'm not sure it is the truth. They are lying.'

Monica Nqabakazi Godolozi, the wife of Qwaqwahuli Godolozi, one of the Pebco Three, and her daughter, Papama, Motherwell, Port Elizabeth, February 1997

Mrs Mtimkulu held up her son's hair, which looked as if it was still attached to part of his scalp. Her husband sat in a corner, his head bowed. The front room of a modest township house. It was into this room that Gideon Nieuwoudt would come to ask the family's forgiveness for his role in their son's death, bringing a camera crew to film the proceedings. Siphiwo's son, Sikhumbuzo (which means 'remembrance' in Xhosa) did not like Nieuwoudt's advances to his family nor did he believe in forgiveness. I watched his arrival on television. He drove right up to the house, armed with a missile, I think it was a brick, maybe a flowerpot. He found his target, took aim, and the camera shook a little as the object flew through the window and connected with the side of Nieuwoudt's head. He reeled. The blood began to gush freely down the side of his face. He looked mortified as he aborted the peace-making enterprise and left the house.

Joyce Mtimkulu's son, Siphiwo, a member of the Council of South African Students, was twenty-one years old and a father of two when he was killed by the security police in 1982. In the year before his death, he had been arrested, detained for six months, interrogated and tortured. Just before his release he was given rat poison in an attempt to kill him and disguise the death as being from natural causes. He was confined to a wheelchair, but was still perceived to be a threat by the security police. Three policemen, Gideon Nieuwoudt, Gerrit Erasmus and Nic van Rensburg, revealed how they had then kidnapped Siphiwo and his friend, Topsy Madaka, interrogated them and drugged them before they were shot execution-style in the back of the head and their bodies burned on a wood pyre. Joyce kept a chunk of Siphiwo's hair, which fell out after he had been fed rat poison during his first abduction by the security police. She refused to believe the accused men when they said they had drugged her son before killing him. She felt that they would never have spared him the terror of knowing that he was about to die.

Joyce Mtimkulu, Zwide, Port Elizabeth, February 1997

Singqokwana Malgas was an ANC veteran who had been imprisoned on Robben Island for fourteen years for his anti-apartheid activities. He had originally been sentenced to twenty-two years but, represented by Nelson Mandela, his sentence was reduced on appeal. While he was in prison, Malgas's house had been repeatedly firebombed and one of his sons had been killed. He suffered a stroke, partly as a result of his injuries from torture, which left him confined to a wheelchair.

When he first appeared at the Truth Commission hearings in April 1996, Malgas avoided describing his ordeal at the hands of the security police. But under questioning by Alex Boraine, the deputy head of the Commission, he finally gave details of his torture. He described the 'helicopter method' in which a mask was put over his face to suffocate him, and then a stick was inserted behind his knees from which he was hung upside down. He broke down during this testimony and tried to cover the 'shame' of his tears with his hands. Archbishop Tutu, who was presiding over the hearings, was so moved that he, too, began to weep. Malgas told the Commission that he would like to tell his torturers, 'If we were only going to get freedom over our dead bodies, I'd like to make them aware we've got freedom.' He died in 1999.

Singqokwana Malgas, New Brighton township, Port Elizabeth, 13 February 1997

Robert McBride applied for amnesty for a number of bombings carried out in his role as unit commander of the ANC's special operations unit. He was responsible for planting a car bomb outside Magoo's Bar on the Durban beachfront on 14 June 1985, which killed three women and left more than seventy people injured. He was sentenced to death three times but released in 1992. In April 1997 he was subpoenaed to appear before the Truth Commission to answer questions about the bombing. Asked whether there had been people in the vicinity of the bar before he left the bomb, he said that he had not been looking out for people, and even if there had been people in the vicinity, it would not have deterred him. He said:

> After the bombing, the thing that shocked me most was seeing the photo of a child whose mother was killed. My immediate reaction was to be obsessed with doing sabotage operations so that I could get rid of apartheid as quickly as possible, because the way I saw it, apartheid was responsible for the tragedy. I'm truly sorry that I caused those three deaths, but this sadness cannot be seen in isolation from the pain and death that apartheid caused to millions of innocent South Africans.

Robert McBride, Pretoria, 29 May 1997

The Bonteheuwel Military Wing was formed in 1985 by a group of politically active high school students from the Cape Flats. These young men, aged between fourteen and twenty-five, were perfectly placed to be recruited by MK, the ANC's military wing. Some were sent out of the country to be trained by the ANC so that they could carry out sabotage operations when they returned. But the unit was easily infiltrated by the security police and many BMW members were arrested, tortured and killed. Mohammed Farid Ferhelst testified before the Truth Commission in Cape Town in 1997. He described how he had once been arrested by twenty-five to thirty armed policemen and on another occasion how he had been tortured in detention:

> I think it was about half past two, the first night in Brackenfell [police station], I heard all the doors opening. Well I was laying in shorts, there was about seven [policemen]. They rushed into the cell, pulled a black bag around my neck, tightened it, cuffed my hands behind my back and took me out, out to the car. In the car they started hitting me. They drove, I don't know where ... for about an hour and a half or so, when they ... took me out again, it sounded like it was in a shack. There I was put in a shower, cuffed to a shower. They started hitting me continuously until I was unconscious. Then they threw water on my face to make me regain my consciousness and like they gassed, teargassed the shower, put me in some bin and they teargassed this bin and started to wet me all over again. Like the majority of the time when they hit you, you didn't even feel the pain because you passed out or something ... After that night, it was every night ... they came to fetch me ... it felt like almost a couple of years, just that short period, because of what people do to you, the way they handle you, the way they hit you.

Later Advocate Potgieter, one of the Truth Commissioners, asked whether he had been able to recognize the voices of any of his torturers. Ferhelst replied:

> In the first and second evenings the bag was over my head, but on the third night, one of the policemen took off the bag. I was virtually unconscious and he then took the rifle and gave it to me and said, 'Why don't you pull the trigger because we are going to kill you anyway?' ... And during interrogation, you make sort of peace with yourself and you realize that what must be must be. To—if I can put it this way, you—you actually prepare yourself for the worst.

Ferhelst escaped death, but the Wing was destroyed by the security police. The idea of transforming a bunch of stone-throwing youngsters into a professional guerrilla team had backfired and left behind a cluster of traumatized young men.

Former members of the Bonteheuwel Military Wing, Bonteheuwel, Cape Town, 15 February 1997
From left: **Abubakr Williams**, **Donovan Fransch**, **Hercules Booysen**, **Qasim Williams** and **Mohammed Farid Ferhelst**

Father Lapsley, a New Zealander, was a pacifist when he arrived at the University of Natal in 1973. 'But,' he explained to the Truth Commission, 'I realized that if you were white and did nothing to change the situation you were actually a functionary of the apartheid government.' He was deported from South Africa in 1976 and went to Lesotho, where he joined the ANC and trained Anglican priests. In 1983 he moved to Zimbabwe, where he was denounced as 'the ANC's chief external ecclesiastical propagandist'. In April 1990, after the release of Nelson Mandela, he received a letter bomb believed to have been sent by a government death squad. He lost an eye and both hands.

It was a normal warm autumn day ... April ... when I became the focal point of all that is evil. I returned from a series of lectures in Canada. A pile of mail had accumulated on my desk, among others something with an ANC letterhead. The envelope stated that it contained theological magazines. While I was busy on the phone ... I started opening the manila envelope on the coffee table to my side. The first magazine was Afrikaans ... that I put aside, I can't read Afrikaans. The second was in English. I tore off the plastic and opened the magazine ... and that was the mechanism that detonated the bomb ... I felt how I was being blown into the air ... throughout it all I never lost my consciousness ... Someone had to type my name on the manila envelope; somebody made the bomb. I often ask the question: 'What did these people tell their children they did that day?' However, the fact that such a sophisticated bomb found its way through the post to me ... I lay sole responsibility for that with F. W. de Klerk. De Klerk knew of the hit squads ... but de Klerk chose to do nothing about it.

Father Michael Lapsley, Cape Town, 16 February 1997

In July 1993 a group from the Azanian People's Liberation Army (APLA), the military wing of the Pan-Africanist Congress, burst in on a Sunday congregation at St James's Church in Kenilworth, a suburb of Cape Town. They opened fire with machine guns and grenades. Eleven people were killed and fifty-eight injured. Letlapa Mphahlele was director of operations at APLA from 1990 to 1993 and ordered the attack. It was a particular blow because it happened after Nelson Mandela's release and the unbanning of all political parties amid negotiations leading up to the first democratic elections. Marilynn Javens's fifty-one-year-old husband Guy was one of those gunned down. She testified at the Truth Commission hearings in Cape Town:

> … it was one of those evenings that we went to church the normal time, started the worship service, and a couple were singing: 'More Than Wonderful' and it was just at the end of that song that the doors opened and I thought it was the wind. And I saw this man standing there and I realized that he had a gun in his hand and he started moving from left to right. I must have still been looking at him without realizing it. In that time my husband went down on his haunches and I realized I had better get down too. And on going down I thought I've got to do something, so I prayed that the Lord would help us, and there was a lot of screaming initially, but even in that there was a kind of peace that I can't even now explain really … Eventually I heard a familiar voice of our Reverend, Ross Anderson, just telling us to stay down … And after a few minutes we got up and—well, I called to my husband and he didn't answer. And I got up and he was still on his haunches and I think I was a bit bewildered at that stage, everybody was milling around and with that an usher came down in front of me towards my husband. And he bent down and obviously … to feel his pulse. And I just said to him, 'Is he alive?' And he shook his head.

Mrs Javens still goes to the same church daily to pray.

Letlapa Mphahlele, Cape Town, February 1997

Dairybelle hostels, Guguletu, Cape Town, 2000

On 3 March 1986 seven young men were shot dead by policemen in Guguletu near the Dairybelle hostels for migrant workers. The case that followed became known as that of the Guguletu Seven. The police claimed the young men were ANC guerrillas and that they had opened fire in self-defence. Three residents of the hostels which overlooked the scene reported that one of the young men had been shot dead whilst trying to give himself up, and another shot dead while lying wounded on the ground. Despite two inquests, no one was found criminally responsible for the killings. The witnesses' testimonies were dismissed and most of the evidence destroyed. In November 1996 the Truth Commission subpoenaed nine policemen from the Western Cape to give evidence about the Guguletu killings. This was the first time the TRC had subpoenaed witnesses to give a public account of their actions. What emerged was that undercover security police from Vlakplaas had deliberately encouraged the setting up of an ANC cell in Guguletu. The young men who had joined it were recruited, trained and armed by black askaris working with the security police. The plan to attack the bus which took policemen to Guguletu every morning had been deliberately engineered and on the morning of 3 March more than two dozen heavily armed policemen lay in wait. The Truth Commission also uncovered secret police files which related to the operation. Their contents included a snapshot of a smiling Senior Superintendent John Sterrenberg, one of the nine policemen, with his foot on the body of one of the dead guerrillas as if he had just returned from a hunting expedition.

One of the young men who died was twenty-five-year-old Christopher Ngewu Piet. His mother testified to the Truth Commission that on the day of the shooting her son's comrades had visited her and informed her that some young men had been shot. She went to the police station to try to obtain more information but was told they had none and she should go to the mortuary, where she found her son's body. She then went home. The news was on television. She explained:

> I saw my child. I actually saw them dragging him, there was a rope around his waist, they were dragging him with the van. I said, 'Switch off the TV, I've seen what I wanted to see. Just switch it off.' ... He had many bullet wounds on his body. After the post-mortem the doctors told me he had twenty-five bullet wounds.

Forensic evidence proved that the young men had been shot at close range.

Ntombomzi Piet, **Mrs Ngewu** and **Cynthia Babalwa Ngewu**, Guguletu township, 22 February 1997

Mrs Miya testified to the Truth Commission on 23 April 1996:

> I am Eunice Thembiso Miya. I have five children; the fifth one is Jabulani, he is the one who passed away on 3 March 1986.

She went on to describe her last meeting with her son. At 4.30 in the morning of the day that he was killed, she had been rushing to catch a train at five which would get her to work at six. (She was a domestic servant.) She said her employer had told her that she had heard on the news that some Russians in Guguletu had been killed. When Mrs Miya got home she and her daughter sat down to watch the television only to see the body of her son displayed as part of the news item.

> No, it can't be him … I prayed, I said, 'Oh Lord … I wish—I wish this news could rewind …' I was told it was just a hand grenade that did this to him, that was next to him. That's the time I collapsed … I don't know what happened after that …
>
> What makes me cry now is that these policemen, they were treating people like animals … But even a dog, you don't kill it like that. You even think that the owner of this dog loves it. Even an ant, a small ant, you think you have feelings even for an ant. But now our own children, they were not even taken as ants. If I say they were treated like dogs, that's not how it happened, I am actually honouring them. They were treated like ants.

Eunice Miya with her grandchildren, Guguletu township, 22 February 1997

30 May 1997

Malan lives in a grand house on the outskirts of
Pretoria. There are hunting trophies pinned to the walls
and Rhodesian Ridgebacks snake around the enclosed garden
protecting their master. The garden smells fragrant. It
is verdant and full of flowering shrubs. Malan is
preparing his defence for the forthcoming TRC hearings
about the South African government's involvement in the
border wars. I thought I detected fear in his eyes under
the peak of his stylish checked hunting cap.

As Minister of Defence from 1980 to 1991 General Malan approved counter-insurgency operations in Mozambique and Angola and was responsible for setting up the 'Civil Co-operation Bureau' (CCB), a covert section of the South African Defence Force responsible for disinformation and assassination. Although National Party politicians did not publicly acknowledge the existence of specially trained death squads, they encouraged the idea that black activism had to be eliminated. In a speech in Parliament in 1981, Malan said: 'As a point of departure we have to accept that the onslaught here in southern Africa is Communist-inspired, Communist-planned and Communist-supported ... They want to establish a dictatorial state for elite black Marxists in the Republic of South Africa ... The security of the Republic of South Africa must be maintained by every possible means at our disposal.' [3]

Despite the testimonies of SADF officers about the direct involvement of senior figures in the Defence Ministry and the Security Council in ordering their operations, Malan has not been found guilty of any crime. He did not apply for amnesty before the Truth Commission, but volunteered to testify. In 1997 he admitted that he had approved the formation of the CCB: 'The role envisaged for the CCB was the infiltration and penetration of the enemy, the gathering of information and the disruption of the enemy.' When asked by one of the commissioners for an example, Malan said: 'Well, sir, you can disrupt the enemy in various ways. You can throw sugar in its petrol.' In fact, the Civil Co-operation Bureau was a secret armed force which operated nationwide. Its actions ranged from the macabre intimidation of Archbishop Tutu, by hanging the foetus of a monkey from a tree in his garden in 1988, to the assassinations of David Webster, an academic and anti-apartheid activist, in Natal in 1989, and Anton Lubowski, a Namibian lawyer and supporter of the South West African Peoples' Organization (SWAPO), in Windhoek in 1989.

General Magnus Malan, former Minister of Defence, Pretoria, 1997

3 Jacques Pauw, *Into the Heart of Darkness* (Jonathan Ball, SA)

Anne-Marie McGregor's son, Wallace, was on a 'call-up' in the South African Army (young men who had completed national service could subsequently be 'called up' for temporary operations) when he was killed in Oshakati on the Angola–Namibian border during operations in northern Namibia in 1986. He was nineteen when he died. Mrs McGregor was presented with his body in a bag and told not to open it but to respect the military code of secrecy. She was told that her son's body was intact. Mrs McGregor testified before the TRC in an attempt to discover the truth about her son's death: was it her son that she had buried and how had he died? After her statement was made public in the media a young man—called 'Michael'—who had served with her son contacted the offices of the Truth Commission. Two commissioners, Wendy Orr and Pumla Gobodo-Madikizela, arranged for him to meet Mrs McGregor and her two remaining sons. In an emotional scene, he related the facts of her son's death. Wendy Orr agreed to keep the personal details of what went on at the meeting quiet. 'What I cannot forget, however, is that as Michael finally came to the point where he described Wallace's actual death, Mrs McGregor said, "So, Wallace *is rerig dood*." ("So, Wallace really is dead."). I realized then that for more than ten years, because she had not been able to see her son's body … Mrs McGregor had been unable to come to terms with the fact that her son was dead. She had sustained the vain hope that it had been the wrong body, that one day she would find him again.'[4]

Anne-Marie McGregor, Paarl, Western Cape, 28 May 1997

4 Wendy Orr *From Biko to Basson* (Contra Books, SA, 2000)

David Zweli Dlamini was subpoenaed to give evidence to the Truth Commission during the hearings into violence between members of the Inkatha Freedom Party (IFP) and the ANC in KwaZulu/Natal. He insisted on wearing a balaclava because he was afraid of revealing his identity as a member of the Caprivi Trainees, the guerrilla unit of the IFP which worked under the cover of the KwaZulu police in the early 1990s. The Caprivi Trainees had been trained by the South African Defence Force to use weapons of war—mortars, light machine guns, AK-47s, hand grenades, anti-personnel mines, landmines and explosives. Everything about their operations was secret; all their instructors used false names. Trainees were called upon to 'wipe out' United Democratic Front or ANC supporters in the Natal area. Daluxolo Luthuli, a former ANC supporter who had switched his allegiance to Inkatha, told the Commission how the houses of ANC and UDF members were petrol bombed at night and when the people inside tried to escape the fire, they were shot.

David Zweli Dlamini, amnesty hearings into Inkatha Freedom Party 'Caprivi trainees', Durban, April 1998

On 5 March 1993 Nkanyiso Wilfred Ndlovu and Mabhungu Absalom Dladla, members of the Inkatha Freedom Party, opened fire on a minibus at Enkanyezini in Natal killing sixteen people. In their amnesty application they claimed that they were avenging the deaths of six schoolchildren who had been ambushed and murdered in the area a few days earlier by members of the ANC. By the time of their amnesty appeal, Ndlovu and Dladla had already been sentenced, but they were called to testify to the Truth Commission. Ndlovu said the crime was motivated by the fact that he wanted to intimidate the ANC so they would stop attacking IFP members. It was discovered later that some of the murdered people were not even ANC supporters. Dladla said he felt 'justified to go and retaliate and pay revenge'. He added: 'The ANC had killed young and innocent children. All these children were the children of the IFP members. Some of the children, three of them, belonged to my cousins.'

Mrs Shezi and Mrs S'thembile Jiyane came to listen to the testimonies of Ndlovu and Dladla. Mrs Jiyane's twenty-three-year-old sister, Bonisile Ngcobo, was among the sixteen people killed. One of Mrs Shezi's and Mrs Jiyane's cousins, Ziningi Mkhize, was left paralysed by her injuries.

Mrs Shezi (left) and **Mrs S'thembile Jiyane**, at the TRC hearings in Durban, 26 March 1998

Mrs Msweli's family were ANC sympathizers and had been feuding with members of Inkatha. Her house had been burned down and the family had gone into hiding. The Mswelis had repeatedly reported incidents to the police but no action was ever taken against the perpetrators. In 1992 Simon, Mrs Msweli's twenty-four-year-old son, was killed and her grandchildren were kidnapped. Mrs Msweli was accused of rounding up people for the ANC. She was threatened and harassed constantly. In 1995 another of her sons, Moosa, was shot dead by police. She has three sons left. At that time it was well known that the South African Police force in Natal was collaborating with the IFP. Mrs Msweli testified to the Truth Commission in Empangeni, Natal, in November 1996. She said her son Simon and his friend had been kidnapped and taken to the Sappi Gum Tree forest. She said the boys had been abducted by members of the 'stability unit' and the KwaZulu police. One of the commissioners asked her: 'Is that were they were shot?' Mrs Msweli replied:

> They were never shot. I think they were assaulted until they died because we couldn't even identify [Simon]. His eyes had been gouged out. He was never shot. He was tortured. He was violated. He was also mutilated. We could not identify him. I only identified him through his thumb. There was a certain mark on his thumb.

Mrs Msweli was asked what happened on the day of her son's funeral. She said:

> We never slept at home on that particular day because the police were frequenting our place and we used to sleep at the forest. During the day or at night they would come and urinate on my child's grave and at times they would mess it up and I would go and report the matter to the police but the police said there was nothing they could do. The very same police destroyed my home and I did not know the reason why they were doing it.

At the end of her testimony, Mrs Msweli was asked what her expectations were from the Truth Commission. She replied:

> I want the people who killed my sons to come forward because this is a time for reconciliation. I want to forgive them and I also have a bit of my mind to tell them. I would be happy if they could come before me because I don't have [my] sons today … I want to speak to them before I forgive them. I want them to tell me who sent them to come and kill my sons. Maybe they are my enemies, maybe they are not. So I want to establish as to who they are and why they did what they did.

Mrs Josephine Msweli, Sappi Gum Tree forest, near KwaSokhulu, where her son Simon was murdered, 6 June 1997

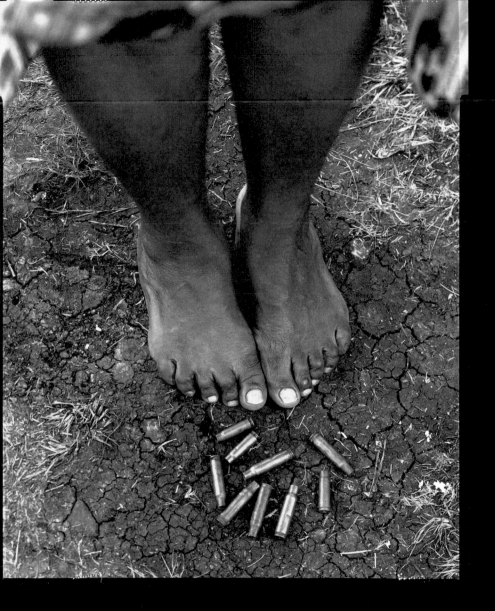

Mrs Mzimela, with the bullets that killed her husband and two of her relatives, near Esikhaweni, KwaZulu/Natal, 7 June 1998

7 June 1998

Bheki Ntuli, a local trade union official from the Empangeni area in Natal, took me to meet three families who had testified before the Truth Commission. One of them was the Mzimela family. Mrs Mzimela told me that in October 1994 her relatives had gathered at her house for a big party. It had been raining. In the distance she had heard the sound of people singing. Suddenly a group of Inkatha 'impis'—warriors—burst in. They opened fire. Her husband and three other men, including a local cattle herder, her cousin, Lucky, and her nephew, Sipho, were shot dead. Mrs Mzimela went into her house and emerged with an old Lion matchbox. It contained the bullets she had picked up after the shooting.

Albertina Mzimela and **Ngoni Siza**, two of Mrs Mzimela's relatives who were present at the Inkatha raid in which Mrs Mzimela's husband and relatives were killed, KwaZulu/Natal, 7 June 1998

Pimville, Soweto, 2000

Maki Skhosana was a twenty-four-year-old ANC activist living in Duduza. She was burned to death in the first officially acknowledged 'necklacing' incident (a rubber tyre is placed around the victim's neck and set alight) in South Africa. In June 1985 a group of young black students in Duduza had been given hand grenades by a member of the ANC and taught how to use them. The students then planned various sabotage missions in the area, including blowing up a local power station. When they pulled the pins, the grenades turned out to be booby-trapped, and eight of them died. Soon afterwards, Maki Skhosana, who knew the boys, was alleged to have been involved in causing their deaths. Against the advice of her family, she insisted on going to the funeral. She was chased by the crowd, stoned and beaten, her clothes were ripped off her and her body set alight. She died next to the grave. Over a decade later, Joe Mamasela, the Vlakplaas operative, admitted that he had infiltrated the group of young students in Duduza and offered them weapons. He had given them a crash course on how to use grenades and they had discussed the blowing up of a power station at KwaThema. The other target was two black policemen. Mamasela had agreed to meet the students at midnight to deliver the arms. Mamasela had then watched the booby-trapped mines and grenades go off as he sat in his car a safe distance away. He was promoted to sergeant after the successful operation which had been named 'Zero Zero Hour'. Survivors of the explosion later told Maki Skhosana's family that Maki had never been party to their meetings, nor had she known of their plans on that particular day.

Evelina Puleng Moloko, Maki's Skhosana's sister, **Diane Moshapalo**, Maki's mother, and
Reverend Moshapalo, Evelina's stepfather, Duduza, Gauteng, 4 February 1997

Evelina Moloko had always protested her sister's innocence. In her statement at the Human Rights hearings at Duduza in February 1997, she described what had happened:

> Maki went to the funeral and I was just pressing my skirt and my skirt got burned. Then I decided that I was no longer going to the funeral and I decided to just go and watch … without participating. Then I went to fetch Dinel [a friend] … [We] were standing on top of a large rock … As we were standing there I felt very cold and I told Dinel that I was getting cold and we should go back home. She was actually surprised as to how I could get cold because that day it was very hot and I made a fire when I got home. Just when I was taking the ashes into the dustbin three girls went past my place. They were shouting slogans and they were saying that they had burned Maki.

She then went to the site where the boys had been buried and found her sister's body.

> … When you look at your sister's body, you do feel it in your own body. You feel something as a sibling. Then I saw her body. I approached her from the feet and I could identify the feet, I could identify her as my sister, but I could not see her face because there was a large rock on her face as well as her chest and I went around to try to identify the body. I was disgusted at the way she was killed.

After she had reported the death to the police, they went to fetch the body.

> I also went home to fetch my little shawl so that I could cover my sister. At that time there were not any people in the streets. I was all by myself. It was as if the whole world had shut itself out and it had shut me out. They brought the body back and I told my uncle that he should cover her, because I did not want to see her body any more and I did not want to see the face.

Evelina Puleng Moloko, the sister of Maki Roselyn Skhosana, Duduza, Gauteng, 4 February 1997
Overleaf: the Truth Commission hearings, Duduza, February 1997

Mxolisa Goboza and Thembinkosi Tshabe, two of the youngest victims to appear before the Truth Commission, described how they had been shot and wounded by police while taking part in a Congress of South African Students' (COSAS) demonstration in Venterstad, on the Orange Free State–Eastern Cape border, in 1993. Goboza, who was eleven at the time, described how they had been *toyi-toying* with a group of students when the police opened fire with pellets and tear gas. Thembinkosi Tshabe, who was fifteen, explained that he had been shot on the same day. Goboza said that he wanted to be a prison warder when he grew up and Tshabe said he wanted to be a nurse or a social worker.

Thembinkosi Tshabe (left) and **Mxolisa Goboza**, Free State Province, March 1997

Anneliese Burgers, Max du Preez and I were having dinner
in Melville. We started talking about Eugene
Terre'Blanche's hairstyle. Anneliese said, 'You can see
he has scraped the long bits over his bald patch. It
looks really weird.' I have this conversation in mind as
I make the long drive to Mafeking from Johannesburg the
following day to attend the amnesty hearings in the
capital of the former 'homeland' of Boputhatshwana. A
large crowd gathers while I photograph Terre'Blanche.
Tension is mounting and tempers begin to flare as a
camera crew tries to film over my head. For some reason
the hairstyle conversation comes into my head again and I
ask Terre'Blanche if he will turn round. (I must have
thought it might produce some revealing and hitherto
unseen image of Terre'Blanche—long greasy strands
scantily covering a bald patch, perhaps.) Quick as a
flash he spits out in Afrikaans, 'ek is nie 'n moffie,
nie.' Taken aback, I can't follow the logic of the
retort. Whatever did he think I might do to him? 'I am
not a homosexual.' I will not turn my back on you.

Eugene Terre'Blanche, the leader of South Africa's extreme right party, the Afrikaner
Weerstandbeweging (AWB), attended the Truth Commission hearings in Mafeking,
in the former 'independent' homeland of Bophuthatswana, in order to oppose the
amnesty application of a SAP officer, Ontlametse Bernstein Menyatswe, who had
killed three members of the AWB in March 1994. In anticipation of the free
elections, and the arrival of what they saw as a 'Communist State', the AWB and
the right-wing Freedom Front were called in to maintain Bophuthatswana's
'independence' against the ANC's plans to return it to the South African nation.
Hundreds of armed AWB members invaded the homeland and in the fighting that
broke out, forty-five people died, including the three who were shot in broad
daylight. In his statement to the Truth Commission, Bernstein Menyatswe said: 'I
killed these men in full view of the members of the media, public and police officers
and members of the then Bophuthatswana Defence Force.' He argued that the killing
had been politically motivated and he was acting in defence of his people and their
right to vote in a national democratic election.

Eugene Terre'Blanche, Mafeking, Northern Province, 23 September 1998

orania

Orania was founded by an alliance of right-wing Afrikaners who, faced with the prospect of a new democratic South Africa, wanted to retreat to their own homeland. They found an abandoned workers' town in the Orange Free State near the Orange River surrounded by farmland. The prefabricated houses had originally been built to house construction workers building a dam on the river. When the dam was finished, the town had been taken over by squatters. One of the first tasks for the new white pioneers was to move out sixty-four coloured families. With financial help from the outgoing government of F. W. de Klerk, the families were rehoused in nearby towns against their will. Orania was opened on 13 April 1991 as a strictly whites-only community. Its policy forbids the employment of any black workers. Everywhere there are billboards which remind Afrikaners to safeguard their heritage: 'Boer Afrikaners Are Proud', 'We Work for Ourselves in Orania', 'We Talk and Think in Afrikaans'. Betsie Verwoerd, the wife of Hendrik Verwoerd, the architect of apartheid and prime minister of South Africa who was assassinated in 1966, moved to Orania soon after South Africa's transition to majority rule in 1994. Her son-in-law, Professor Carel Boshoff, played a prominent role in Orania's development. She died in February 2000, at the age of ninety-eight.

Monument to Hendrik Verwoerd, Orania, September 1997

The Le Roux children, residents of Orania, September 1997

30 September 1997

I feel distinctly uncomfortable staying in this White Homeland. Everything seems tainted. It is bleak, isolated and deathly quiet. The 'Whites Only' sign at the entrance says it all. In the museum built to honour Hendrik Verwoerd, I view the suit in which he died. He had been stabbed several times by Demitrios Tsafendas, a Greek parliamentary messenger. The ripped suit is displayed proudly on a mannequin inside a glass case. When I sign the visitor's book I notice Nelson Mandela has been there not long before me.

Esther Le Roux, a secretary at the Freedom Front, the right-wing Afrikaner alliance party, had left a comfortable Cape Town suburb to move with her husband and their four children to this new white paradise. Asked if she felt she was isolating her family, she replied, 'How can I be isolated when the future is here? With God's help we will build a Volkstaat. I'm sure of it, maybe not in my lifetime, but certainly that of my children.' [5]

Betsie Verwoerd, the wife of Hendrik Verwoerd, Orania, 30 September 1997

5 Russell Miller, Night and Day, the *Mail on Sunday*, 31 October 1997

P. W. Botha, the former Prime Minister of South Africa (from 1978 to 1989), refused to co-operate with the Truth Commission. Eventually he was subpoenaed and appeared at the Magistrates Court in George, the small town in the Eastern Cape where he has lived since his retirement. The local ANC office planned a large protest to highlight the crimes and injustices that had been committed during the Botha regime. Botha, who was eighty-two years old in 1998, gave a defiant press conference before his hearing and later stormed out of court, shaking with rage and shouting, 'They want to destroy my image and through me to humiliate my people!' Damning evidence was heard implicating him in crimes committed during his time as South Africa's leader. The Truth Commission wanted to question the former Prime Minister in particular about his role in chairing the State Security Council which had directed undercover operations during the 1980s. The Truth Commission's executive secretary read out extracts from the minutes of Security Council meetings which ordered 'the identification and elimination of revolutionary leaders, particularly those with charisma'. Another document ordered the 'physical destruction of the revolutionary organisations, to wit, people, facilities or funds, inside the country or out, by any overt or covert means necessary'. The aim was 'to make the rotten areas clean before they became too infected. To establish that requires a lot of violence from our side, regardless of the international reaction.'

ANC supporters, George, Eastern Cape, 22 January 1998
Overleaf: Riot provisions, George, 1 June 1998

Roger ('Jerry') Raven was the explosives expert responsible for the letter bombs that killed Ruth First in Maputo, Mozambique, in 1982 and Jeanette Schoon and her six-year-old daughter, Katryn, in Lubango, Angola, in 1984. Both women were staunch supporters of the ANC and were living in exile from South Africa. Ruth First, the wife of Joe Slovo, chief of staff of Umkhonto weSizwe, the military wing of the ANC, and head of the South African Communist Party, was working at the university in Maputo; Jeanette Schoon, who was married to another long-term ANC member, Marius Schoon, had been moved with him to Lubango from their home in Botswana by the ANC for their own safety. The killings were masterminded by Craig Williamson, a SAP double agent who had infiltrated the ANC network and was on good terms with the Schoons. Raven, who was a member of the security branch of the SAP, explained in his amnesty application that he had been trained as part of his job as an intelligence agent and had carried out the manufacturing of the bombs under Williamson's orders. He tried to persuade the commissioners that it was possible for him to have made the Schoon bomb and fitted it into the envelope without noticing who the letter was addressed to and without leaving any fingerprints. He said:

> At the time in 1982 or 1983, I can't remember the date, Craig Williamson instructed me to assemble two IEDs [Improvised Explosive Device] in the form of letter bombs, A4 size. He gave me no indication as to who the targets were. This was the standard operational procedure when it came to 'Need To Know'. Only after the media reports of the death of Ruth First and Jeanette Schoon and her daughter and the congratulations of Craig Williamson, did I suspect that the two IEDs I had constructed were responsible for their deaths.

In his amnesty statement, Raven explained: 'Williamson said that the letter [that killed the Schoons] had been intended for Marius Schoon, but that it served them right.' In September 1998 Brigadier Willem Schoon, a member of the South African security forces, applied for amnesty for the attempted murder of Marius Schoon in Botswana in 1981.

Roger 'Jerry' Raven, amnesty hearings Pretoria, September 1998

Brigadier Willem Schoon was a former head of C section, the anti-terrorism unit of the South African Police security branch responsible for liaising with the commanders of the undercover unit at Vlakplaas such as Dirk Coetzee, Jack Cronje and Eugene de Kock. He applied for amnesty for his involvement in numerous cases of murder and abduction, which included the deaths of two ANC activists in 1972, two PAC members in 1981, the attempted murder of Marius Schoon in 1981 and 1982, the abduction of the ANC activist Joe Pilly from Swaziland, where he was living in exile, the death of the human rights lawyer Griffiths Mxenge in 1981 and the deaths of Jeanette and Katryn Schoon in 1984. Brigadier Schoon denied his direct involvement in the murders. He was also implicated in the bombing of the Congress of South African Trade Unions (COSATU) headquarters in Johannesburg in 1987. In November 1998 he told the amnesty committee in Pretoria:

> I am not a murderous person, although it might look that way. But we were forced to participate in these actions by the circumstances that prevailed at that time.

He received amnesty and is retired.

Brigadier Willem Schoon, amnesty hearings, Pretoria, September 1998

Marius Schoon was a committed member of the ANC. He and his wife Jeanette were considered high-profile targets by the South African intelligence personnel for several years before they were resettled in Angola by the ANC. There had already been attempts to assassinate Marius Schoon in Botswana in 1981 and 1982, and the letter bomb that had killed his wife and daughter in 1984 was intended for him. At the time, the South African media attributed the bombing to an internal struggle within the ANC. He returned to South Africa at the beginning of the 1990s and worked for the Development Bank. He remarried. When Craig Williamson and Brigadier Willem Schoon applied to the Truth Commission for amnesty for the murder of his wife and daughter, Marius Schoon fought to have it refused. (Brigadier Schoon admitted that he could be related to his intended victim, but he did not consider him family because he was on 'the other side of the fence'.) Marius Schoon attended the hearings in Pretoria in September 1998 with his son, Fritz, who was two years old when his mother and sister were killed. Marius Schoon died in February 1999 before hearing the outcome. Williamson, Willem Schoon and Raven were all granted amnesty for the Schoons' death.

Marius Schoon, Johannesburg, 18 January 1998

Craig Williamson, known as the 'apartheid superspy', was a former police officer who joined military intelligence and headed the Security Branch's foreign section. He applied to the Truth Commission for amnesty for the murders of Ruth First and Jeanette and Katryn Schoon, and for the bombing of the ANC's London headquarters in 1982. Williamson had been a double agent since his early twenties. Already a member of the South African Police force, he enrolled in 1972 as a student at the University of Witwatersrand in Johannesburg and became heavily involved in anti-apartheid politics. By 1976 he was vice-president of the National Union of South African Students (NUSAS). He left for Europe in the same year and worked for the International University Exchange Fund (IUEF). Jeanette Schoon was also active in student politics and knew Williamson. After 1977, when she and Marius Schoon were banned from South Africa, Williamson stayed with them at least once in their house in Botswana. In 1980 he was recalled to South Africa to head up the military section of the security police in Pretoria. He described to the Truth Commission how he had 'commissioned' the letter bomb which killed Ruth First and how, two years later, the order was repeated:

> ... early in 1984 I was given an instruction to go to the office of Brigadier Piet Goosen, my group head, and he had with him in a large envelope a communication, a postal item which was I believe an intercepted communication between the ANC in Botswana addressed to Marius and Jeanette Schoon in Lubango, Angola ... [he] asked me if I thought that Jerry, that is Warrant Officer Raven, could make a similar device to that which had been sent to Maputo and which had killed Ruth First to replace the contents of this communication. I told the Brigadier that I would request Jerry to see what he could do.

Williamson claimed that when he heard Schoon's wife and daughter had been killed six months later, it felt as if 'a cold bucket of water' had been thrown over him.

George Bizos, the lawyer acting for the Slovo family, questioned Williamson about his attitude towards the bombings:

> Bizos: And you didn't care whether the right victim was killed or his wife or their child?
> Williamson: ... When you say I didn't care whether the right victim was killed or his wife I have to concede that it made absolutely no difference to me whether Joe Slovo had been killed—in fact I'd say probably I would have thought it better if he had been killed—it made very little difference to me whether Joe Slovo was killed or Ruth First was killed or Jeanette Schoon was killed or Marius Schoon was killed, but I never in my life targeted an innocent child.

Craig Williamson, amnesty hearings, Pretoria, January 1998

General Johann Coetzee was Commissioner of Police in Pretoria between 1978 and 1985. He came to the Truth Commission to seek amnesty for the bombing of the ANC offices in London in 1982. Craig Williamson testified that he had a 'long and very close' association with Coetzee, under whom he had served as a police spy in the 1970s. Williamson said, 'I would never have done anything that General Coetzee didn't approve of.' Coetzee was the direct superior of Brigadier Piet Goosen, who had asked Williamson to order the letter bombs that killed Ruth First and the Schoons. When faced with evidence linking him to their deaths, General Coetzee refuted all knowledge of any involvement with any assassinations committed by any of his personnel while he served as Police Commissioner. Throughout the amnesty proceedings he argued about the definitions of certain words, even challenging the meaning of 'eliminate', saying that it did not mean 'to kill'.

During the hearings, Coetzee was asked by George Bizos, the lawyer acting for the Slovo family, why the police failed to arrest anybody for the assassinations carried out during his term as Commissioner.

> Bizos: Now you can't tell me of any planned and executed assassination where the police succeeded in finding the culprits. Is this because you were incompetent or because you turned a blind eye, or because you as a Security Force, as Intelligence Services, as Army, actually planned them ...? Of the three alternatives, which do you choose? Or perhaps you can think of another one ... I'll repeat my question: Was it incompetence, was it turning a blind eye or was it overall complicity?
>
> Coetzee: I would choose, Sir, in a certain respect, incompetence.

General Johann Coetzee, former Police Commissioner, Pretoria, September 1998

Colonel Eugene de Kock, commander at Vlakplaas between 1985 and 1993, was known amongst his colleagues as 'Prime Evil'. He and his group of trained killers were responsible for some of the worst atrocities committed during the apartheid years. He entered the police force in 1968 at nineteen. Ten years later he joined the Security Branch at Oshakati on the Namibian border and in 1979 became a member of Koevoet, the SAP's counter-insurgency unit responsible for the deaths of hundreds of SWAPO members in South West Africa and Angola. Koevoet employed a 'bounty system' under which its members were paid for those they killed.

De Kock returned to South Africa and joined the unit at Vlakplaas in 1983. As commander he was directly answerable to his superior, Brigadier Willem Schoon. For the next ten years de Kock was in charge of groups of trained askaris and his units carried out numerous killing raids and ambushes of alleged ANC and PAC guerrillas. These included Zwelinzima Nyanda, a former MK commander, in Manzini, who was shot in Swaziland in 1983, Johannes Mabotha, who was blown up with explosives at Penge Mine, Burgerfort, in 1989, nine people who died in Maseru, Lesotho, in 1985, and three ANC activists who were murdered in Mbabane, Swaziland, in June 1986. After this last operation, de Kock drove to the home of Johann Coetzee, the Commissioner of Police, at 5.30 in the morning and reported to him, and to Brigadier Schoon, that the job had been done. In his amnesty hearing, Johann Coetzee denied that he had ordered the raid, but he did not deny the visit:

> As far as I remember … something like twelve or more members came to the house … It was the kitchen, my wife made coffee for them, they stood around … they showed me the documents [which they had taken in the raid] and those people with me in the kitchen I congratulated, I said: 'Chaps, that was a job well done, to bring for instance these documents, to have a shoot-out.'

De Kock was also responsible for organizing the 1987 bombing of the COSATU headquarters in 1987 and the 1988 bombing of Khotso House, both in Johannesburg. He alleged that the order for the COSATU bombing had come from Prime Minister P. W. Botha.

The unit at Vlakplaas was disbanded in 1993. In 1994, only days after the democratic elections on 27 April, de Kock was arrested. His trial began in 1995. He faced 121 charges of which nine were for murder. In September and October 1996 he was found guilty of eighty-nine charges, including six for murder, and sentenced to 212 years in prison plus an additional two life sentences. In May 1997 he applied to the Truth Commission for amnesty for over sixty incidents ranging from fraud to multiple murder. He received amnesty for over fifty of them, but amnesty was refused for three cases, which meant that de Kock will remain in prison for life. Not one of the commanding officers who gave de Kock orders has been charged.

Eugene de Kock (centre), Amnesty hearings, Pretoria, 1998

Ferdi Barnard, a former policeman, was a 'freelance' member of the Civil Co-operation Bureau (CCB), the secret unit of the SADF established in the late 1980s, when the fight against the ANC was being intensified. The CCB's aims included the 'elimination' of ANC and other anti-apartheid activists, the disruption of organized revolutionary groups and the covert gathering of intelligence from international companies. Barnard was a well-known figure in the Johannesburg underworld. He managed a brothel and was a heavy cocaine user. In September 1997 he was arrested and charged with the murder of the academic and human rights activist David Webster, who was shot dead in Natal in May 1989. He also faced twenty-two further charges of murder, attempted murder and the illegal possession of firearms. Barnard was involved in a CCB attempt to murder the advocate and SWAPO member Anton Lubowski (he was later shot dead in Windhoek, Namibia, on 12 September 1989), and the human rights lawyer Dullah Omar, leader of the United Democratic Front, who survived to become Justice Minister in the new government. (Barnard was also responsible for hanging the monkey foetus outside the home of Archbishop Tutu in 1988.) Barnard is serving a life sentence for the murder of David Webster. It was he who reportedly gave his friend Eugene de Kock the name 'Prime Evil'.

Ferdi Barnard being returned to Pretoria's maximum security prison, 19 March 1998
Opposite: Barnard's inscription, written for his prison warder, in a book about South Africa's security operations

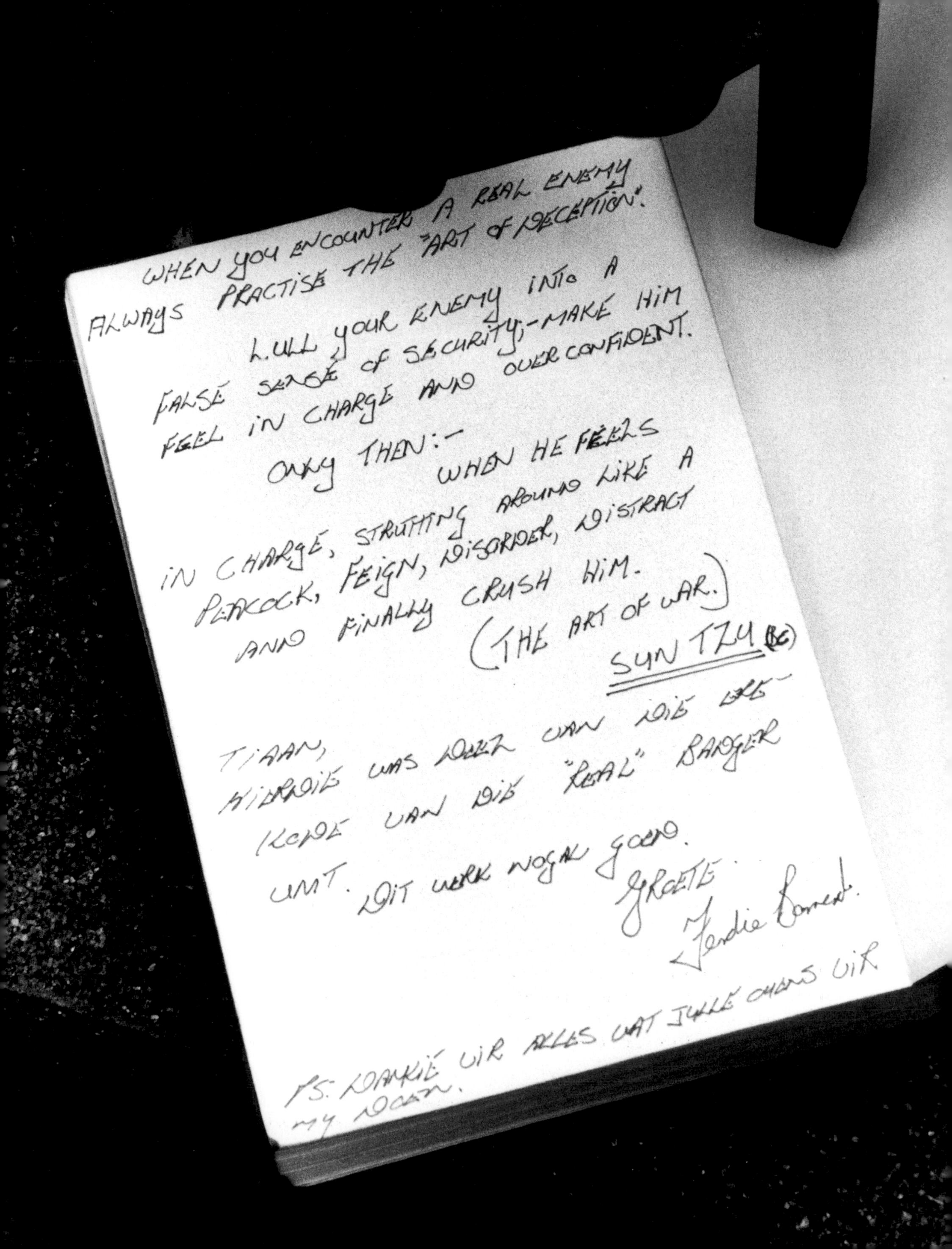

WHEN YOU ENCOUNTER A REAL ENEMY

ALWAYS PRACTISE THE "ART OF DECEPTION".

LULL YOUR ENEMY INTO A FALSE SENSE OF SECURITY,—MAKE HIM FEEL IN CHARGE AND OVER CONFIDENT.

ONLY THEN:—

WHEN HE FEELS IN CHARGE, STRUTTING AROUND LIKE A PEACOCK, FEIGN, DISORDER, DISTRACT AND FINALLY CRUSH HIM.

(THE ART OF WAR.)

SUN TZU (BC)

TIAAN,

HIERDIE WAS MAAR VAN DIE IDES WAT KOME VAN DIE "REAL" BANGER UIT. DIT WERK NOGAL GOED.

GROETE

Ferdie Barnard.

P.S: DANKIE VIR ALLES WAT JULLE GAANS VIR MY DOEN.

I arrange to meet Wouter Basson in a park called Magnolia
Dell near his favourite restaurant, Huckleberry's. It's a
pretty setting—weeping willow trees and strutting ibises—
but there has been a summer shower and the light is poor.
Jeffrey, my waiter, says Wouter and his family come to
Huckleberry's every Thursday at 5 p.m. 'He likes hake,
grilled, and rock shandy.' Wouter arrives promptly. I go
to greet him. He comes up close and says in a low voice,
'I hate you. I really hate you.' Why? 'Because I agreed
to do this. I am going to disappear you,' he says. 'I
will vanish you and your family.' A pause. 'No, only
joking.' I picture him in a wizard's hat and think of my
family in London as he asks for my address. Despite this
we proceed with the picture. 'I'm battling with the
light. Give me light,' I say. 'Well, that about sums it
up,' he replies. 'Crappy light and a murky situation.' I
assume he's referring to his past.

Wouter Basson, an ex-South African Army Brigadier and cardiologist, was the
founder and head of 'Project Coast', the Army's secret biological and chemical
warfare programme which was based at Roodeplaat laboratories north of Pretoria
between 1981 and 1993. Nicknamed 'Dr Death', he went on trial in Pretoria in
October 1999 charged with sixty-one counts of murder, conspiracy to murder,
possession of addictive drugs and fraud. He pleaded not guilty to all the charges.
He refused to apply for amnesty but was called to give evidence to the TRC's
enquiry into biological and chemical warfare. The TRC heard evidence about the
manufacture of 'murder weapons' such as food and cigarettes contaminated with
anthrax, milk contaminated with botulinum, poisoned chocolates, poison-infused
T-shirts and poison-tipped razor blades. It was alleged that the programme had
supplied SADF undercover units with muscle-relaxants which had been administered
to SWAPO prisoners of war (they were given overdoses of the drugs and then
thrown out of aircraft into the sea); that research had gone on into mass distribution
of a vaccine that would sterilize the black populace and into bacteria that would
affect only black people. Research was also going on into alternative methods of
crowd control using drugs such as Mandrax, Anthrax, LSD, Ecstasy and marijuana.
In 1992 a commission ordered by President de Klerk found Basson guilty of
'unauthorized activities' and forced his early retirement from the army. Basson was
re-hired by the ANC government as a cardiologist at Pretoria Academic Hospital.
In January 1997 he was arrested for the attempted sale of approximately 100,000
Ecstasy pills. In May 2001, as his trial continued, he was dismissed from his hospital
post. A spokesperson for the Ministry of Health said: 'In the light of his activities
and the charges against him, the department does not find him fit to serve in it.'

Dr Wouter Basson, Pretoria, November 2000

Spitskop, near Upington, Northern
Cape, about 200 miles south of
the Namibian border, sunrise,
31 October 2000

On 10 November 1985 in Paballelo just outside Upington in the Northern Cape, a residents' meeting about poor conditions in the township spiralled out of control. A group of young men gathered on the football pitch and began to dance and sing. The police intervened and several days of rioting followed. The next day a pregnant woman was shot and killed by police, who alleged she had been committing acts of violence, and on 12 November over 3,000 people from Paballelo assembled on the football pitch to protest. After ten minutes the police threw tear gas canisters into the crowd and began to break it up. Some of the protesters retreated down the street where Lucas Tshenolo Sethwala, a black policeman, lived. They threw stones at Sethwala's house, breaking the windows. Sethwala retaliated by shooting and badly wounding a young boy called Dawid Visagie. When Sethwala left his house he was attacked by the crowd, who beat him and then poured petrol over his body and set it alight.

Three weeks later twenty-six people were arrested and charged with the crime of public violence and 'common purpose' in bringing about Sethwala's death. At their trial in 1986, fourteen of them were sentenced to death. In 1988 a team of lawyers from Cape Town and Windhoek, led by Anton Lubowski, appealed on their behalf. In May 1991 the appeal court in Pretoria overturned twenty-one of the twenty-five murder convictions and dismissed all fourteen death sentences. Only four people were sentenced to prison terms for public violence. Anton Lubowski was assassinated in 1989 while the case for appeal was being prepared.

When the Truth Commission visited Upington in October 1996 they heard testimonies from Evelina de Bruin, Accused no. 18; Zuko Xabandlini, Accused no. 6; and Xolile Yona, Accused no. 20.

Zuko Xabandlini, Accused no. 6, Upington, Northern Cape, October 2000

I took a small plane to Upington far up in the Northern
Cape to meet and photograph one of the former accused,
Evelina de Bruin. Her story was particularly tragic. She
and her husband Gideon Madlongolwane had both been convicted
of murder, though she denied being at the scene of the
killing. She was nearly sixty and had ten children when she
was sentenced to death. The two youngest were eight and
ten. On death row she declined physically and emotionally.
She was given a Bible, but she could not read. Evelina felt
guilty and anxious about her children, alone in the world
without her support and guidance. We got to the township to
discover that Evelina had gone to another town to bury a
relative. There was no message. Her house was empty. Inside
I could see a plaque which read: *Wat is 'n huis sonder 'n
moeder?* What is a house without a mother?

Evelina de Bruin testified before the Truth Commission in Upington, 2 October 1996. Justice Jan Basson was the presiding judge at the murder trial in 1986.

My friend, my husband, Gideon Madlongolwane, is not here next to me. He died last month. He was buried last week. He is dead today for the way he was treated in jail. But I knew inside that I should come here and tell the truth. The truth that there is a Judge Basson who will never see the heavens. They are shut, totally closed to him.

Since I was born, I have never seen the doors of prison. I was in the court and heard [Judge] Basson saying he would sentence us. I did not understand what he was talking about. I saw people crying. People were throwing themselves on to the floor, people were fainting. In Pretoria, when I got there at sunset, I heard the truth of my sentence. I was shocked when I saw Yolile [Yona] and my husband, they could not even walk because they were handcuffed and there were cuffs on their legs. They were undressed, naked in the streets. I was taken to the women's prison and given a glass of water. I refused. I was not thirsty for water but I was thirsty for the truth.

The evidence that was given in court was deceptive but our new President, talking about the Bible, says we must forgive each other. He says that we must throw these previous burdens into the Red Sea. I hold no grudge but I have pain. In Pretoria, they brought a rope, about a metre long, and put it around my neck. I think they wanted to know whether this rope was going to fit. They measured my neck and they recorded [it]. I want to declare that both my husband and I were sentenced to death whilst innocent. Do they, do they think that we are mad? Do they think we are going to kill somebody else's son? That is all I have to say.

Hennie Smit's eight-year-old son, Cornio, was killed in 1985 by a bomb blast in the Sanlam Shopping Centre in Amanzimtoti, Natal, just before Christmas. Four other people were killed and over sixty injured. Three MK members were arrested and sentenced to death. It was claimed that the bomb had been planted in retaliation for a raid by the security forces on an ANC base in Maseru, Lesotho, which had killed nine people. The three MK members were executed.

Hennie Smit spoke very movingly about how, after one of the bombers, Andrew Zondo, had been hanged, he had gone to visit Zondo's parents to console them. He told the Truth Commission that at first he hated all blacks for killing his son, but now he had come to realize that his son was a hero of the struggle who died so all South Africans could be free. Mr Smit became an outcast in his own white community in Pretoria:

> I told newspapers that I thought my son was a hero, because he died for freedom ... he died in the cause of the oppressed people. A lot of people criticized me for this. They thought I was a traitor and they condemned me. But I still feel that way today.

Mr Smit lives in Pretoria where he buried his son. He breeds doves and repairs broken television sets.

Hennie Smit with his dove, Snow White, Pretoria, May 1997

Press room, Jiss Hall, Johannesburg, October 2000

'Brood' Van Heerden, a former Vlakplaas operative, was giving evidence about rape, torture and alleged murder dressed in a casual light-blue safari suit—shorts and a short-sleeved shirt. His victim wept with her memories and he sat tapping his feet, slightly agitated and sometimes stone-faced as he listened. Why was he nicknamed Brood, I wondered (*brood* means bread). Somebody said it had to do with the shape of his head. I pictured him as a cartoon character—enlarged loaf-like head, protruding nose, gangly legs and an outsize pair of shorts. In his testimony to the TRC he said, 'If the person does not co-operate then you torture the person until he co-operates.' When asked why the police had to remove the clothing of detainees, he said, 'to break morale and demoralize a person'. Through my headphones, the translations sound like a strong heartbeat in the background. 'I played open cards with the Commission,' he said. 'I came with the truth from day one. I am the one being sacrificed. Why am I the one being beaten now?'

Later I came across this empty press room with the television playing to nobody. It felt like a symbol of the gradual winding down of the whole, long, truth-seeking mission.

I want to look at what happened;
That done,
As silent as the roots of plants pierce the soil
I look at what happened,
Whether above the houses there is always either smoke or dust,
As there are always flies above a dead dog.
I want to look at what happened.
That done,
As silent plants show colour: green,
I look at what happened,
When houses make me ask: do people live there?
As there is something wrong when I ask—is that man alive?
I want to look at what happened,
That done,
As silent as the life of a plant that makes you see it
I look at what happened
When knives creep in and out of people
As day and night into time.
I want to look at what happened,
That done,
As silent as plants bloom and the eye tells you: something has happened.
I look at what happened
When jails are becoming necessary homes for people
Like death comes out of disease,

I want to look at what happened

Mongane Wally Serote
OFAY-WATCHER LOOKS BACK

Gathering firewood near the Dube hostels, Soweto, 2000

exhumations

One of the immediate results of the Truth Commission hearings was that some of the perpetrators, particularly members of the white security police and the SADF who confessed to the abduction and murder of anti-apartheid activists, disclosed where the bodies of their victims were buried. For the victims' families, many of whom had waited years, not knowing what had happened to their spouses, their parents or their children, this was often the first confirmation that their missing relatives were actually dead. Once the locations were known, exhumations supervised by officials from the TRC took place all over South Africa.

Dawie Botha, undertaker, Vlakplaas, March 1998

17 March 1998

In November 1985 three young ANC guerrillas were killed by security police and taken to Abraham Grobbelaar's farm at Boshoek to be buried. Thirteen years later the crowd wait patiently in the hot sun amid the stench of death and the uncertainty. Instead of three corpses, the grave yields up twelve, sealed inside black plastic bags. The unidentified bodies are numbered A1, A2, A3 and so on. The digging stops when the sun begins to set. The gruesome task would be resumed the following day.

Exhumation at Boshoek, near Rustenburg, Northern Province, March 1998

Unidentified corpses exhumed at Boshoek, March 1998

Constable Brian Ngqulunga was an askari working with the security police at Vlakplaas under the command of Colonel Eugene de Kock. He died on 19 July 1990. In 1996 Captain Wouter Mentz, a former Vlakplaas officer, applied to the Truth Commission for amnesty for a range of murders including that of Ngqulunga. He had been killed because he was suspected of passing information back to the ANC. Mentz testified that he and three other security branch men had abducted Ngqulunga, beaten him, shot him with several rounds from an AK-47, then dumped his body, which had been discovered by the regular branch of the police (the post-mortem result showed that his tongue was missing when the body was found). When the police informed the unit at Vlakplaas that one of their men had been killed, de Kock had arranged for Ngqulunga to be given a proper police burial at a remote site on the farm with a cross to mark the grave. After Mentz's testimony, the grave was reopened under the supervision of officials appointed by the Truth Commission. Ngqulunga's remains were buried in a heavy metal coffin which had to be prised open. It took almost two hours before funeral parlour employees could force the cement block covering the grave to move.

Brian Ngqulunga's wife, Tholakele (far right), supported by friends, Vlakplaas, March 1998

Funeral parlour worker at Brian Ngqulunga's grave, Vlakplaas, March 1998

Bridgett and **Frans**, **Brian Ngqulunga's** children, with a relative, Vlakplaas, 1998

Brian Ngqulunga had been deeply disturbed by his work as an askari for the Vlakplaas commanders. According to Joe Mamasela, a fellow askari and friend of Ngqulunga's who later gave evidence to the Truth Commission against his former Vlakplaas colleagues, Ngqulunga had been unhinged by the organized murder he had been involved in. Mamasela said: 'It disturbed him. He was a completely devastated person. The whole exposure worked into his mind. He was frail, he drank too much and he was on the verge of a nervous breakdown.' It was after a drunken binge that Ngqulunga went home and shot his pregnant wife three times. She survived, and after the exhumation she waited, ready to take her husband's remains back to Soshanguve, the family home, for a proper burial.

Tholakele Ngqulunga, at her husband's grave, Vlakplaas, March 1998

Tholakele Ngqulunga with **Fanie Malapo**, an investigator of exhumations for the Truth Commission, Vlakplaas, March 1998

Workers leaving at dawn, Onverwacht ('Unexpected') resettlement camp, Orange Free State, 1984

AUTHOR'S ACKNOWLEDGEMENTS

For my mother and my father

Special thanks to:
Max du Preez for his great help and friendship; my children Gabriel and Savannah; Anneliese Burgers, Gail Regon, Shenid Bhayroo, Antjie Krog, Jacques Paauw, George Luse, Lavinia Brown, John Allen, Archbishop Desmond Tutu and all the Truth Commissioners, the media liaison officers, especially Mdu Lembede, Phila Ngqumba, Christelle Terreblanche, Mbulelo Sompetha, Vuyani Green, Meleny Burts and Terry February, the TRC translators, Gisele Wulfsohn and Mark Turpin, Jane and Vanessa Raphaelly, Carrie Raphaelly and Lenny Stoch, Andrew Meintjies, David Crookes, Laura Cave, Susan Blank, Tertius Meintjies, Gillian, Robyn and Shawn Slovo, Mark Holborn, Kathy Ryan, Maggie Davey, Bheki Ntuli, Myner Bovu, Anita Roddick, Clive Boursnell, Tom Miller, Peter Gabriel, Annie Parsons, Simon Esterson, Neil Burgess, Alice Wynne Willson and all the staff and photographers at Network, Selma and Marco Alexander, Nigel Horne and Martha Richler, Russell Miller, Mark Gevisser, George Bizos, Nyame Goniwe, Nombuyiselo Mhlauli, Anton Ackermann, Dirk Hartford, Gavin Hartford, Julia Rabie, Andrea Durbach, Neil Stemmet, Mike Barnardo, A. V. Fish, Frank Cairns, Millie Simpson, Mark Pringle, Jann Turner, Ursula and Martha Thomas, Neil Ross, Luke Foreman, Justin Patrick, Albie Sachs, Roger Friedman, Priscilla Naidoo, Benny Gool, Nceba Ezra Singapi, Nkosinathi Biko, Johno's Darkroom, Danny Chau, Beith, Matter & Weich, Polaroid, David Weyman, John Rivett and Pete Louw, Robin Bell, Elaine Proctor, Reshada Crouse, Sophie Harrison, Gillian Kemp, Margaret Staker, Peter Dyer, Michael Ignatieff, Pumla Gobodo-Madikizela and the editor of Granta magazine, Ian Jack. Finally to Liz Jobey, my editor, who gave this book so many of its words and so much of its shape and purpose.

I would like to thank all the people who told me their stories and allowed me to photograph them.

SELECT BIBLIOGRAPHY

BORAINE Alex, *A Country Unmasked*, Oxford University Press UK, US 2000

DURBACH Andrea, *Upington*, Allen & Unwin, Australia 1999, US 2000

DE KOCK Eugene with Jeremy Gordin, *A Long Night's Damage*, Contra Press SA 1998

KROG Antjie, *Country of My Skull*, Jonathan Cape UK 1998, Times Books US 2000, Random House SA 1998

MANDELA Nelson, *Long Walk to Freedom*, Little Brown (Abacus) UK 1994, Little Brown US 1995

ORR Wendy, *From Biko to Basson*, Contra Press SA 2000

PAUW Jacques, *Into the Heart of Darkness*, Jonathan Ball SA 1997

Siyaya!, Issue 3, Spring 1998, Idasa publications SA,

SCHWARTZMAN Adam, Ed., *Ten South African Poets*, Carcanet Press UK 1999

The Truth and Reconciliation Commission of South Africa Report, Vols 1-5, Macmillan Reference UK 1998, 1999; Grove's Dictionaries US 1998, Juta SA 1998

USEFUL WEBSITES

The official Truth and Reconciliation Commission site: www.truth.org.za
The African National Congress site: www.anc.org.za

1/06 ⑨ 1/05   I/II· 10 4/04
6/16 ⑬ 5/16

Copyright for the text and photographs © 2001 by Jillian Edelstein
Introduction copyright © 2001 by Michael Ignatieff
'Memory and Trauma' essay copyright © 2001 by Pumla Gobodo-Madikizela
All rights reserved.
No part of this book may be reproduced, in any form, without written permission from the publisher.

Extracts from *Long Walk to Freedom* by Nelson Mandela. First published in Great Britain and the United States in 1994 © 1994 by Nelson Rolihlahla Mandela. Reproduced by permission of Little, Brown and Company.
Ofay-watcher looks back by Mongane Wally Serote. First published 1972 © 1972 Mongane Wally Serote. Republished in *Ten South African Poets*, ed. Adam Schwartzman, Carcanet Press, 1999. Reproduced by kind permission of the author.

Originally published in the United Kingdom by Granta Publications, 2001
Published in the United States by The New Press, New York, 2002
Distributed by W. W. Norton & Company, Inc., New York

ISBN 1-56584-741-5
CIP data available.

The New Press was established in 1990 as a not-for-profit alternative to the large, commercial publishing houses currently dominating the book publishing industry. The New Press operates in the public interest rather than for private gain, and is committed to publishing, in innovative ways, works of educational, cultural, and community value that are often deemed insufficiently profitable.

The New Press, 450 West 41st Street, 6th floor, New York, NY 10036
www.thenewpress.com

Book design by Peter Dyer

Printed in Italy

2 4 6 8 10 9 7 5 3 1